Tales from the Red Carpet

LIZZIE CUNDY

Tales from the Red Carpet

SO
HO
FRIDAY

Soho Friday Media Ltd.,
3-4 Temple Bar Business Park,
Strettington Lane, Goodwood,
Chichester, West Sussex,
PO18 OTU

www.sohofriday.com

www.facebook.com/soho.Friday
twitter.com/@sohofriday
www.instagram.com/sohofriday/

First published in hardback in 2019

1 3 5 7 9 10 8 6 4 2

British Library Cataloguing-in-Publication Data:

A catalogue record for this book is available from the British Library.

ISBN: 978 1 91309 400 3

Design and typesetting by Phoenix Media
www.phoenixmediadesign.com

Printed in the UK under supervision of Jellyfish Solutions Ltd

Papers used by Soho Friday Media Ltd. are natural, recyclable products
made from wood grown in sustainable forests. The manufacturing processes
conform to the environmental regulations of the country of origin.

Every reasonable effort has been made to trace copyright-holders of
material reproduced in this book, but if any have been inadvertently overlooked
the publishers would be glad to hear from them.

To my sons

My boys

To whom I owe everything in my life and my world

And to all those who are searching for love but have yet to find it,
never give up hope

Contents

Acknowledgements

"It was about 7 years ago that Lizzie's name was first brought to my attention when a previous client told me she was looking for new management and they thought I should sign her. 'Oh no,' I said, fearing she might steal my husband, 'she's one nipslip away from nuttydom isn't she?'

It was another year or so before our paths actually crossed at a red carpet event. Initially I was impressed by her professionalism as she expertly interviewed the client I was with - no detail was overlooked as he unwittingly opened up to her on camera. But it was later that night it happened, BOOM! It was over cocktails and her bowl of nuts that I fell in love with this unexpectedly vulnerable, funny, kind, clever, crazy woman. I soon realised she had spent years being used by 'hangers-on' exploiting her generosity and incredible black book of contacts even Paris Hilton would kill for! I vowed that night to change all that: to make people see the real woman behind the lashes and lip gloss... or die trying!

I fully intended to save her, but in hindsight, I think she saved me.

Now we speak everyday, and everyday we keep each other grounded in this bonkers business we call 'show business'. And she makes it a better place that's for sure."

Vickie White – Lizzie's manager

There are so many people I need to acknowledge but it is simply impossible to mention you all. I do, however, need to single out Vickie White my manager.

When you fall in love at first sight?

Well, that's what happened when I first met Vickie, who came into my life and transformed it. She never once stopped believing in me and loved me, as I did her, from the very start.

And I will never forget our Jerry Maguire moment. Thank you.

My dear mum. Your kindness got me through and I want you to know that.

And to all my friends who stuck by my side, loyal to the end, you know who you are and I'm truly blessed to have you in my life.

Thank you.

Lizzie

Co-author's note

I worked with Lizzie to put this book together spending hours chatting face to face with her, or on the phone. What I can tell you is Lizzie is not Lizzie Cundy. Like Dame Edna Everage what she portrays on purpose is a caricature of herself, her alter ego, designed on the whole to simply earn a living. But it's not an ordinary living of course which you will soon see when you read about her meetings with Tom Cruise, Al Pacino, George Michael and hundreds of other celebrities.

Whilst I knew her a bit before we started to write this book together in the winter of 2018, this is not the woman you think you know and not the woman I imagined I knew. The flow of this book has changed many times over the weeks. She is even more famous than you would think and she is pretty famous already. If you search her name on the internet there are an astonishing 1.9m entries and I only got to page 18 on Google for my research so I have no idea what the other 1.899m entries say. But, knowing what I know now, most of what is written online would be either wrong or just an extension of the caricature she has deliberately made of herself.

This is essentially a story of a woman's fight back after her marriage break-up, how she has managed to do that and keep a family together at the same time. And how she has begun a new search for love, sidetracked by the incredible list of multiple A-list celebrities she has met. The story in some parts is one of heartbreak, but she is nonetheless certainly not heartbroken. She is a very happy person and she spreads positive energy whenever she enters a room, it really doesn't matter who you are, she will be the same towards you.

Lizzie must be one of the most well-connected people in this country. I think socialite is a good word for her now, WAG is definitely not. She can seemingly fix or sort any problem for a friend and her blagging skills are jaw-dropping and have been for the best part of 35 years.

In helping Lizzie write this book I have interviewed numerous friends of hers and there is a common theme amongst them. She is simply a bloody nice person and they are hugely protective of her.

The book cuts out very large parts of her life with her ex-husband, which as the relationship lasted 23 years doesn't seem the cleverest thing to do in an autobiography.

But it is done on purpose because those years did not define her, the ones in this book did.

Richard Johnson

Exclusive Content

For the first time in book publishing history, a film has been made of the 'making of the book' which shows the fascinating interaction between Lizzie and Richard Johnson, the co-author, as the book is put together. You can see how the discussions turned into the actual words, and how they debated endlessly what should or should not appear. The dynamic between them is hilarious, but equally fascinating. Halfway through they actually fall out, as Richard, a heavyweight in the UK publishing industry and author of the bestselling book *Show me your Medals*, doesn't hold back in his opinions.

Full details of how to get the 30 minute documentary are at the end of the book.

Also, for the first time in publishing history, during the course of reading this book you will see these:

behind which are short clips from the film, and show you how an extract from that page was put together. This is the actual footage of the discussions that led to the words you will read. Nothing is staged and is filmed with a basic camera set up, with no one else in the room.

All you have to do is put your phone into camera mode as if you were about to take a picture, but instead place your phone screen over the code you see (like the one above) and the link will pop up onto your device ready to watch, free of charge.

This is Lizzie totally raw and uncut.

Prologue

I locked '9 and a half weeks' Hollywood hellraiser Mickey Rourke into the boot of the Mercedes, checked my make-up in the wing mirror, hot-wired the car and drove off into the rainy, dark London night.

And that my darlings is a very true story.

Immediately you will think, well, what you are thinking?

And who could blame you? I haven't helped the public's view of me over the years.

If you Google my name, 17 of the first 30 pictures that appear are of me in racy outfits, sometimes even in the very depths of winter. Putting Mickey into the boot of my car, and everything that piece of imagery gives, captures the opinion many have of me. But it's not as it seems. Just like my life.

I first met Mickey in 2010, through a mutual friend Cheryl who ran Blakes hotel in London where the Oscar nominated, BAFTA award winning superstar, was staying. I interviewed him for ITV and the headline soundbite was that he told me he had slept with 14 women in one night. It made the headlines the next day as this was the period when footballers sexual antics were big news everywhere. And knowing Mickey as I now do, I believe the '14 women' story and it may not even have been his record.

Following the interview, I arranged a £25,000 photoshoot for him with OK! magazine owned by my terrifying friend Richard Desmond. The photo crew duly arrived at Blakes, set up and then we all had this feeling that something was missing. That 'something' turned out to be Mickey himself and I was dispatched to his room to come back with a full reconnaissance report.

The reconnaissance was easy. I could hear him inside his room. As I banged on the door getting more and more angry, an unrepentant but naked Rourke opened it and said:

"I don't feel like it honey, sorry, it's been a long night."

Behind him was a naked blonde who looked contently satisfied. Looking down I could see why. When it looked like I was about to burst into tears, he stared at me with his wolflike eyes and in his mind doing ME a favour says:

"Oh, ok Trouble I will come down but I want the 25 grand in cash and I want it on my bed in the next 30 minutes."

At this point I only had one thought. Not how the bloody hell was I going to get 25 grand in 30 minutes, not how on earth was I going to explain this one to Richard Desmond, but instead I had this very simple question:

"Why on the bed? Did he have some sort of cash fetish? Would the blonde rub the cash all over him in a bizarre form of holistic massage?"

Speechless at both the request and the sight in front of me, I retreated back to the corridor for thought and closed the door. I realised immediately that I needed more clarity from him but it probably wasn't appropriate to knock on the door again, walk in, interrupt him and the blonde by saying:

"So sorry to trouble you darling, but would a mix of fivers and tenners be ok and I will get a VAT receipt for accounts won't I?"

I ran downstairs, found Cheryl and explained my plight. With a knowing look, she beckoned me into the hotel office and there in the corner was what could only be described as a gangster safe, a big old glamorous thing that had seen better days. Which was therefore exactly like me then. Cheryl looked around, so I looked around too in a spy type of looking around way, but feeling very important at the same time. We then nodded wisely at each other and she opened it, slowly, very slowly, very, very slowly. It may have been done for dramatic effect, which if it was, was definitely working on me. I needed to wee and have a vodka in equal order of priority.

Inside the safe it was like an adult wonderland of wonder. She picked out some cash but didn't count it, she seemed an expert just like Mickey as he didn't count it either when I delivered it all to him 5 minutes later.

I'm not sure if I was disappointed or relieved when he simply got dressed and came with me to the photoshoot. He wasn't a sexually depraved cash deviant after all and was a total professional from that moment onwards. I must have made something of an impression though because I met up with him a year later when he came over for the 2011 BAFTA's. After the ceremony we went for a nibble in Nobu which turned into several nibbles very quickly. Joe Calzaghe the boxer was with us so we had a nibble ménage à trois.

It was getting late, Joe had left and just as we were headed out it was clear trouble loomed as the paparazzi were starting to gather outside. Mickey was worried that he and I being seen together wouldn't be great news to explain to his current Russian girlfriend, even though nothing had happened between us and nothing was going to in my mind, despite 'Mr 14 a night' looking so cool in black jeans, T-shirt and long swept back hair.

"Come with me darling" I purred to him, "my car is parked around the back, we will leave that way. You can hide in the boot."

Which I like to think sums me up. Not only am I utterly crazy but I have a heart of gold to match it. I saw nothing wrong in shoving an Oscar nominated actor into the back of my car rather than doing the obvious which was to call a cab to come around the back for him.

Didn't even enter my head, I just wanted to help a friend. As I always do.

As he got into the boot and snuggled down like Rourkey the Rooster, I jumped into the driver's seat like it was the opening scene from Starsky and Hutch and hot-wired the car. It was the only way it would start, I had lost the keys some time before. Don't ask where I learnt how to do that but I can disclose now, exclusively, it wasn't from the nuns at my boarding school.

I drove off to his hotel, again Blakes, which is in Kensington. With reasonable traffic it would be a 10 to 15 minute journey from Mayfair. About 5 minutes in I heard the unmistakable sound of a police siren coming up behind me and then the officer on his police motorbike indicated that I must pull over. In a 'I must be guilty of something' innocent panic, I went quickly back over what I had drunk that night which was just one vodka tonic. I didn't have to worry about drugs because apart from a few joints I have never taken any in my whole life.

The policeman, despite my flirting, did not believe I wasn't drunk and so called a unit to breathalyse me, which took 40 minutes. And all that time, Mickey Rourke, Oscar nominated Mickey Rourke, was stowed away in the boot of my car.

You can just imagine what the headlines would have been the next day if he was discovered:

'Man-eater Cundy kidnaps Rourke and is confident of beating 14 times a night sex record.'

'Rourke hides from Cundy as even he couldn't keep up with her!'

Or from The Guardian:

'Lizzie helps the environment by car sharing with her friend.'

As I stood there it went through my head "What would I say if the police opened that boot?"

The best plan I came up with was to act all innocent and virginal and say, "Blimey, that's a turn up for the books isn't it officer?" as Rourkey ran away into the London night in search of lucky lady 15.

Throughout the whole 40 minutes wait, I tried to whisper messages to Mickey but the officer was having none of it and told me to not move. In a rebellion against authority, which is frankly not unusual for me, when he wasn't looking I tried my best to get close to the boot. But it was like the Hokey Cokey. One step in, one step out. I probably should have shaken my boobs all about, I may have distracted the policeman enough to get close to the car.

I eventually took the breath test, passed (I'd like to think with an A grade) and was set free into the rainy London night. I was soaked and dying for a wee but I did the British stiff upper lip thing and as coolly as I could, walked in a 'dying for a wee like way' back to the car.

And then of course hot-wired it when the police weren't looking.

So, there I am driving like a nun in a hot-wired car, a screen legend in the boot who I'm not sure is dead or alive and following me, as they knew something was amiss but couldn't quite place what, were two metropolitan police officers on motorbikes. What do you do in these circumstances? What you normally do on the way home? Call your friends and start chatting about the latest wedges? Put a bit of Club Tropicana on and start singing?

Instead I did what I had been doing all my life, through some incredibly dark times. I issued my rallying call, which in years to come I'm sure will be hailed by famous scholars of the time as comparable to Henry V at Agincourt and anything that Churchill wrote in the second world war:

"Come on Cunder's you can get through this."

I had said that same call to arms to myself when my husband cheated on me. It was cried out when I was given the slipper by the nuns at school, followed by my knuckles being whipped just for their pleasure. It was said when I tried to come out the other side of an eating disorder at 16 brought on by the horror of being nearly raped by a well known showbiz manager, and it was repeated again and again when my best friend committed suicide causing the whole world I knew to cave in around me.

And that night I did get through it. Because somehow, I always do.

The police eventually decided they had better things to do and sped away. A few minutes later I pulled up, not far from Blakes as I didn't want the concierge to ask me if I had any bags to take out of the car which I would have then replied:

"No bags my darling, but here is ten pounds, can you get Rourkey out of the boot for me?"

I walked towards the back of the car with panic rising to the levels of giving birth and to my utter relief, there he was, Hollywood's finest, alive, and looking like he had just slept in the boot of the car. Which is what he had just done of course all the way since leaving Nobu.

He got out of the boot, nonchalantly brushed himself down, gave me a 'What the hell just happened' look, clicked his fingers at me and with total charm said in that American gravelly, deep, sexy, cool, Manhattan accent:

"Y'all have a great evening honey" and strolled into the hotel.

And that is why, my darlings, he is Hollywood box office.

Wembley Grass

"The dynamic between Lizzie and her children is amazing to witness and her two boys are simply the nicest kids, so laid back, so loving to their mum.

I first met Lizzie after my break-up with Grant Bovey in 2013, and we have such a deep bond now. This isn't an air kissing or just an occasional dinner type of friendship, it is the real deal. She has a key to my place and many times I just find her there when I get home.

Lizzie is like a sister to me now.

I think the Shirley Valentine TV show she did in the summer of 2018 showed her more vulnerable side, but she has come out of it a more rounded person. It showed the side of her that said she would do anything for anyone and I know she can't resist that, quite often at the detriment to herself.

She earns her living by being 'brand Lizzie' - it's as simple as that and that is how she puts a roof over her head. That's always what is uppermost in her mind, to earn a living for her boys so they can benefit from it. She does it all for them and always has done it all for them. Sure, her lifestyle will be perceived as incredible but looks can be so deceptive, it's mainly a job. She isn't being a party girl, she is being a grafter and that's probably difficult for someone not in the business to accept, which I totally get, but it's true nonetheless.

Lizzie always wants to see the good in someone, and isn't the sort of person who looks for an argument no matter how serious the issue is.

She shows great dignity in everything she does, especially when her marriage broke down.

Most of all, what people should know about her is that behind the facade of the racy outfits and nights out, stands a hard-working mother and an exceptional one at that."

Anthea Turner – very close friend and TV celebrity

It had been such a lovely summers day at a friend's party in late August 2010 and I was driving home.

I had just passed the Chelsea FC ground, Stamford Bridge, when I got a call from a very close friend of mine. I pulled over because she just didn't sound her normal self at all and I was naturally worried. It wasn't her I should have been concerned about though, because she proceeded to tell me that which deep down I had known for a while, but my heart had been blocking. What she revealed to me was that Jason, my husband, was having an affair with an opera singer who I shall just call Madame Butterfly. I didn't ask her how she knew, or any of the details, I just instantly knew it was true.

I had confronted him about the rumours six months before and he had said there had been a short fling with someone but that it was over, it was a mistake. I just wanted to save our family, save our future, so I accepted it, believed him and threw myself into my work. But it had obviously continued.

I could hardly breathe but I didn't cry. I was numb. I was in shock but the whole realisation sweeping over me as I sat there wasn't shocking. Because I knew that he would carry on with it. Deep down I already knew. He had been strange for the last few months, distant, and as I sat for just a few terrifyingly lonely minutes, it all started to make sense to me. That's why he was late back those nights, that's why he said he kept missing trains, that's why it was difficult to get hold of him recently and in just 180 seconds of eerie summer silence outside Stamford Bridge, I worked out precisely the answers I had been seeking.

I knew. At last, finally, I knew.

Speeding down the A3 towards our Hampshire home I just felt worthless. We had been together 20 years and the memories came flooding back to me in a tsunami of total and utter grief. In 1990 when we had first met, I was just 22 but a successful model already with a very promising career ahead of me. I was attracted by his sense of humour and not his dress sense as he wore white jeans on our first few dates, a clothing addiction you probably needed to check into The Priory to cure yourself of.

He was an up and coming football player for Chelsea but hadn't broken into the top tier then, which meant I was likely earning far more than he was at that stage. I was happy to put my career to one side though and become a devoted partner to him. When he eventually broke into the first team, a year after our first date, I watched all his games religiously through rain or snow. The problem was, those games were few and far between. Frustratingly, he kept getting injured and worse still he was diagnosed with testicular cancer in 1997 just at the point his career looked like it was really taking off. My job of course was to be strong for him and strong for the family which I was during the day, but there were many nights I simply cried myself to sleep with worry.

In the end he had a 10 year first team career which ended in 2000, the year our second son James was born, our first Josh arriving 3 years earlier. But he had long periods of time out from playing during those years and I nursed him through every one of his medical problems, abandoning my own working dreams in support of his working dreams.

Despite being a great player and leader, solely because of the on/off injury issues, Jason did not get the awards, trophies and international caps he deserved. I have absolutely no doubt he would have done with better luck, I'm not going to change history now despite what happened. He was *that* good.

Living with an injured football player isn't easy but I believed in marriage and the vows that you make that day. I had given everything to him, simply everything, and driving down the A3 in the late summer's afternoon haze, all that now seemed to have been for nothing.

I began to think about my father who had died at the age of 69 some years before. On our way to the church on my wedding day, he could sense something wasn't quite right as only your parents really can I suppose.

"You don't have to go through with this my darling" he said, holding my hand in the car that day, and before I could really reply he asked the driver to pull over and took me to the only logical place we could think of to talk properly. A pub. As hilarious as that image appears in your mind now darlings, of a bride propping up the bar with a vodka in her hand, putting the occasional pound into the fruit machine and tucking into a bag of pork scratchings, it was a very meaningful moment.

We talked about everything. It was hugely emotional. At the end, I looked him in the eye and said I wanted to be married and I wanted my husband to be Jason. Looking back, I should have played on the fruit machine longer.

Getting off the A3, I finally arrived at our house on that sad August day and I could tell by seeing his car, that he was there as were my two sons. I walked in. He just looked at me and I just looked at him. He realised what was in my head, what I had discovered and he gave me a knowing look before saying:

"You have taken your eye off the ball" as if all this was my fault.

My eye off what ball exactly? Had Nike just released a new one that said it's ok for a married man to cheat on their wife? Oh yeah, that one, silly me.

He growled some unrecognisable words at me and despite the kids now realising what was happening, he stormed upstairs, grabbed an armful of clothes and shoes and walked out of the door to his car, skidding away in his Porsche like a 17 year old who had just taken delivery of his secondhand Ford Escort.

It had been a fast and furious 10 minutes since I had walked into the house and yet a totally cold and unreal experience. There had been no shouting from me, no questions from me. He just couldn't wait to get away, he didn't want to face reality and didn't want to face the boys.

He ran away to his new lady. And to make that point even more, he didn't contact me or his children for a month afterwards. He had been a hero figure to the boys up until that moment, but now the dynamic suddenly changed.

It appeared the grass wasn't just greener, it was like Wembley Stadium's pitch and he was no doubt mowing it 3 times a night, spraying the lawn feed around everywhere, while his wife waited for her husband to call.

Jason had apparently met Madame Butterfly on a train journey back from Cheltenham races in the spring of 2010 and according to reports, she did the chasing that day. I didn't know the truth then and I don't know it now either. I never asked. It was what it was. As the boy racer wheel spun away, what was obvious was that it was over and the soprano had no doubt yodelled the final act of Figaro for all it was worth whilst having sex with my husband behind my back.

When he left the house, I just immediately locked the door. I have no idea why, it just felt like the right thing to do. The children were the only thing on my mind, their well-being and their emotional protection. I just wanted to wrap my arms around Josh and James, to love them like never before. They were only 16 and 11. The numbness I felt would be nothing compared to what they would feel, and I told them right away all that I knew about what was going on. But I didn't rubbish Jason to them and never have done. It was not a great moment though. It was simply heartbreaking. I faced that moment alone. One parent taking responsibility. One.

To break the ice that night we watched Alan Partridge and we laughed. A laughter of sorts. We didn't speak about it anymore, we all had our own thoughts. Our own private reflections. That night I lay awake as the clear moon and I bonded, counting every single star I could see, then did all that again as I tried to work out what the hell should happen next. But I knew that my world as I knew it was over. And that was what I was in such a state about, the familiarity of routines would change, everything normal would become abnormal.

I didn't 'wake' the next morning as I didn't sleep. I simply dragged myself out of bed and called my mum. I had a new series of my ITV show to do that day but I had no energy or soul left in me to do it.

My mum in her usual determined way, simply, but firmly told me:

"Darling don't let him win. Stop feeling sorry for yourself Elizabeth, it's the kids who should feel sorrow. Put your make-up on, put your lip gloss on and get out there for them."

Which I did, and to this day I continue to do.

During those first few weeks apart, the only way I knew he was actually still alive was because I could hear his voice on Talk Sport the radio show he did after his football career had ended. But arrangements had to be made for the kids and I had to start getting on with my life.

However, there was an elephant in the room which still had to be dealt with.

I was friends at the time with the Coronation Street actress Shobna Gulati, and ironically just before I split with Jason she had told me there were two ways to get over a break-up.

"To get over a man you have to get under a man or failing that, throw his stuff into a skip."

As it was only 7 days since my husband had left, I was naturally still in my 'all men are lying, cheating, bastard sons of pigs' phase, so I would rather have poked sticks in my eyes and run naked through the village street, than have another man 'under me' right then. So, I did the next best thing, called the plant hire company, invited two of my closest friends around and we were all soon staring at a skip parked on my front drive.

What else was I supposed to do? He wasn't calling me and I had to do something, I couldn't live in a house with his things around me. At the appointed hour, my oldest school mates Helen, Linda and Michi turned up, but as I opened the door they were all wearing face masks with Jason's face printed on them, which was one of those laugh or cry moments in life. They stuck them to the side of the skip and off we went upstairs, systematically removing my old husband from the new world he had forced upon me.

In-between large glasses of rosé, we carried out of the house all his clothes, his shoes, his life and threw it away. Into a skip. I looked for his white jeans to laugh at one more time, but he probably still had them on as they were nowhere to be seen. There were no throwing things out of the window in drama, no cutting up of his trousers, no burning ceremony as the ladies danced to 'I Will Survive' by Gloria Gaynor. Every time I saw his face on the side of the skip I just got more determined and thought, fuck you. I didn't feel anger, I just felt inner strength. It was liberating. And right there and then I planned to survive.

Later on, as I was sat down on the sofa I realised that there was one more thing which needed to leave the house. What had started off as a symbol of love and eternity had now turned into a symbol of lies and despair. I walked to the skip, didn't stop for any reflection and simply threw my diamond wedding ring on top of the rubbish. Diamonds are not forever but a marriage should be.

And for good measure, a week later still feeling rebellious, I changed the carpets as well.

Sometime after *skipgate* he eventfully found out what we had done, the only thing he got into a real state about was the loss of his José Mourinho's football bible which apparently detailed the training methods he has used. That told me two things right away. This weak man was no longer the strong man I had married and he had obviously taken his white jeans away when he left as he never asked after them that day.

About 4 weeks in, I got a call from the press saying they had been following Jason for some time and they now had pictures of him and her together. A lady from the Daily Mail even turned up on my doorstep to reinforce the point and basically said, "Tell us what is going on because we are going to print it anyway, so it's surely better to get your side of the story out there too." I was always taught by the former Sun editor Stuart Higgins who was a good friend, to deny, deny, deny, which is therefore what I did, and shut the door firmly closed on the reporter. It was then that the scarlet pimpernel Jason Cundy finally called me after a month of grass cutting silence, because he had got the same message from The Mail as I had. So, it was the press calling him that seemed to break his silence, not his desire to know how his two sons were. Jason was keen on us having a united front with regards the media, but I didn't want to talk to him, it was now about to become public knowledge and I couldn't take it all in.

When I put the phone down on him, it's the only time in that whole period that I really cried. Really shed tears. Not for him, for me. The pressure of it all. The pressure of keeping myself together for my children. His children.

I literally crumbled onto the floor for the first and only time. Grief encompassed me. The feeling of rejection was soul destroying and my God, it was a very tough period. I hadn't just lost him, I had lost all his family too and I had never felt so utterly alone.

I very quickly stopped eating and drank too much. Nothing made sense anymore except I had to look after my boys because he was making no attempt to. My career needed to keep going, and it was obvious he was going to be patchy on long-term support as he had never previously been generous on anything. I was living on adrenaline, and had no sleep night after night. I wanted my boys not to suffer, to have the same nice things as if nothing had changed at all. I wanted them to see their mum strong for them, "Don't worry guys I'm here, stand with me." Behind that, I was falling apart and so I went to the doctors who prescribed me sleeping pills and anti-depressants.

My legs were like Twiglets, I was not looking after myself. My decline was obvious but when I got home from the doctors, and just before I was going to take a pill, I heard my father's voice as I looked at them all laid out on the kitchen side.

"You don't need them. You need strength that comes from you. Not fake strength, inner strength. Stand up and be a mother."

And within a minute of walking into the house, I threw them away. From that moment, it was just me, no chemical help as my assistant.

There was only one time during that first raw six months where I regretted my actions. Up to that point I believe I had shown real dignity over the adversity thrown at me. I had been invited to the Royal Opera House a few months after the split, and I was told Madame Butterfly wasn't going to be in it, so off I went with Helen Fospero from GMTV and some other friends. I had no interest in stalking anyone, I had not made any contact with her at any stage since the break-up.

However, when we arrived and the opera started it was clear I had been badly informed.

There she was tucked away in the back of the chorus line but I recognised her straight away. In the interval Jason came storming over to my group and demanded to know what we were doing there and was I going to cause any trouble? Which frankly I wasn't until of course he asked me that question and wound me up. Emotions were running high, I had had a few drinks and as he walked away I launched a mushroom vol-au-vent at him which I didn't see land, but Graham Norton told me later it had hit Jason slap bang in the middle of the forehead.

Naturally the press picked up the story and reported it a few days after. I didn't really care though and the headline was an all-time classic:

'The opera singer, the WAG and the flying vol-au-vent.'

Some people in a break-up 'stalk' the other side, search for reasons. I can understand why they do it, why shouldn't they? But I didn't do that. I have only ever really met Madame Butterfly once some years later when we had to discuss arrangements for the children. I also never 'stalked' Jason after the break-up. Why? Because very quickly after we split I simply didn't care about the reasons and it wasn't going to eat me up. He had already taken 20 years of my life he wasn't going to take the next 20. People fall out of love all the time, it's not a crime. He saw something in her he didn't see in me. Fair enough. I quickly saw many things in men after the separation I never saw in him. It works both ways.

One of the early decisions I took, surprising my friends, was to keep my surname as Cundy. Which may seem like one of life's worst decisions ever, as it's hardly the greatest showbiz name or indeed greatest any name, but I did it for this simple reason, which has nothing to do with him. It was because I wanted my children to have the same name as me so there was no confusion at the school gates, no explaining to do at parents' evenings.

Many times over the years I have reconsidered that early decision, should I 'rebrand' to my original name Lizzie Miller, but I am comfortable with the conclusion I took in 2010 and have stuck to my guns ever since. So, a Cundy I remain. Or to be more precise, the Cundetta aka Cunders, aka Cunderella. Or, as was the case once on South African TV which I will explain later, please welcome onto the stage - Lizzie Cunty!

The roots of the marriage break-up stemmed from 2007 onwards. It was then time for me to be myself after so many years where I had stood by him as the 'Victorian' wife. The work baton had now passed to me and I wanted to be my own person. A relationship cannot stay the same forever, it evolves to fit the circumstances.

Did I take my eye off the ball? Footballers get lots of attention in various ways. When he was playing he did too. Many girls want to be with a footballer and most footballers love that thought, deep down, and temptation is everywhere for them. Peter Crouch, the England player, was asked the question once:

"If you hadn't been a footballer what would you have been?"

and he replied...

"A virgin."

When Jason was playing, I recognised that his was a special career, one where they get so much adulation from the crowd, from women and indeed their clubs who arrange the players day-to-day life for them, that it stands to reason a wife is probably going to need to mirror this in some way just to 'compete'. I made the decision that I would be like that for him and be there all the time for him when he was playing. No one forced me to do it, Jason didn't force me to, I did it because I recognised the reality if I didn't. Many people in my situation I am sure would have done the same thing.

In 2010 when we split, he wasn't a professional footballer anymore but he still acted a large part of the time as if he was. 10 years after retiring.

By 2010 I had changed, compared to say 1998, when I did everything for him. So, in that respect I had taken my eye away, but the ball was not the same any longer and our lives had moved on, so I had too. My needs now became just as important as his. They always were of course, but I had put them to one side for years and years. I worked very hard in the 12 months or so before we split, and he felt that my lack of 'attention' then gave him an excuse for an affair.

And, of course, any attention from a new woman will beat the 'attention' from a wife of many years hands down every time.

The simple fact at the end of the day is this. He made the conscious decision to cheat on me in 2010. I didn't cheat on him, ever.

Case closed in any moral debate.

And my thoughts at this moment on Jason? Well, in fairness, I rarely think about him to be honest, and haven't done for years. He doesn't deserve a piece of my emotions any longer. I would hope though, looking back, he would have done things differently with regards us all and I believe to be honest, he probably would have done. One day he may get off his high horse and say that, who knows. But frankly now, who cares.

For him and I though, as soon as he walked out of that door in August

2010 we were done and so the time had come for me to search for love once again.

And it came to me quicker than I imagined it ever would do.

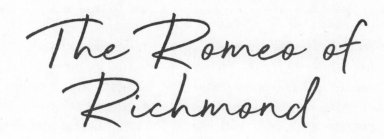

The Romeo of Richmond

"I have known her for 11 years or so, and I think there is more than one 'Lizzie'. She portrays a caricature version of herself. The real Lizzie has been the same all the way through our friendship.

I met her in a bar I used to own in Wimbledon called SWNineteen, and we hit it off immediately as she seems to do with most people she meets. We organised the 'WAGs fashion show' which was an unbelievable event, raising money for the cancer charity she was heavily involved with at the time because of Jason. We actually closed down Wimbledon Village High Street that night because of the press and paparazzi. I had her posing on top of a very large and expensive motorbike outside the bar on the pavement!

I know she did a lot to try and save her marriage at various points in the months before the break-up. She tried for her kids.

I have seen over the years people gravitate towards her like a light that moths are attracted to. If anyone needs her help she will try to create openings or pathways for them to get into the business, she is kind and really wants to help. There is just something totally remarkable about her. Fake friends are everywhere in her life and can be takers, they never return any favours to her and I think she is now starting to see that for herself.

I nickname her 'last minute Lizzie'. She is always late, and always late to give an invitation to an event.

She knows how to be part of the media circus. She knows all the paps by name and genuinely likes them. She knows they earn a living from their photographs, and always stops for them. It's all a bit of a game but she probably knows how to play it better than anyone, and I have seen her contacts list grow and grow over the years to what now must be one of the most connected people in this country.

I loved her on Shirley Valentine in the summer of 2018 as many of my friends have told me how lovely she came across. So like the real Lizzie who is just exceptionally funny."

Susie Homes – long-term friend, co-organiser of the WAGs fashion show and owner of Red Carpet Entertainments.

It was in 2007 that I first saw him, 3 years before my split with Jason.

We were at a Halloween party that autumn and in walks this phenomenally handsome man. And when I say handsome, if you take Zeus on a scale of 1 to 10 and reckon he would be a 9.8 in good looks, this man was at least a 12. Or 14.

I'm not sure if you will remember the cheeky girls, but those cheeky little ladies were with him for some reason when he walked into the party, and he seemed very proud of that fact - the cheeky little boy! As he walked past, he tapped me on the shoulder and said "You are too good for him" pointing at Jason in the distance and walked away. Just like that. He then spent much of the rest of the night looking at me but he always seemed to be smiling no matter who he was looking at or talking to. He had an incredible happy energy about him.

But I had no idea at all who he was.

The next evening, I was at the Pizza Express in Richmond with Nicky Sedgley, wife of Steve who played for Spurs, waiting for Jason to turn up and join us for dinner. Jason didn't show and I didn't know where he was despite numerous calls I made to his phone and to his friends. At that moment though, in walks the cheeky guy from the previous night and to show his bravado wasn't a one-off moment of bravadoism, he sat down at the very table next to us.

He then introduced himself more formally this time and said:

"You are Lizzie aren't you? I'm Danny I said hello to you last night."

I had never met anyone as confident as this, even beating me into a poor second place of pure cheek. He wasn't arrogant though in that pompous sort of way, just naturally very sure of himself and an expert at being charmingly friendly.

I went to the loo and as I came out he was there pretending it was just a coincidence he happened to be loitering outside, right at that very moment studying the plants.

"Can I take your number Lizzie, I am an apprentice at Wasps Rugby club and I hear you are very well connected. I need some help with my management and general advice."

Which was simply the worst chat-up line ever but was actually very true. He did need help. His full name was Danny Cipriani and with some reluctance I took his number rather than give him mine and said I would do my best to put him in touch with someone.

Pretty much immediately after that 'meeting' he started to take the UK rugby scene by storm making his full club debut. I thought he was in his late 20's but it turned out he was actually just 20. I happened to be talking to my friend Stuart Higgins a week or so later, the former editor of The Sun who was now in sports management, and he was going on and on about this star the whole of the UK seemed to be interested in.

"My God everyone is after this player, he is a maverick, so talented but obviously not getting looked after properly. He is the next Jonny Wilkinson, maybe even bigger, he is very, very special."

I asked innocently "Who are you talking about?" and he said "Danny." I told him I knew him, and that he wanted me to help him out if I could.

"Lizzie, do you realise you have the crown jewels in your hands, would it be possible to arrange a meeting with him?"

Which is what I did and Stuart started to manage him. It was just a favour I did for both of them I didn't get any money for it, why would I want to? That didn't please Jason though who was seemingly needing to monetise everything I did at that point as he searched for a profitable career after football.

Having set up Danny with Stuart in a plutonic match made in sporting heaven, I turned my attention to a men's cancer charity event I was organising and thought I would try and get the Wasps Rugby team involved. I knew Danny could sort it as he was fast becoming the star player, which he duly did. But with 24 hours to go he got on his egotistical high horse and said he wasn't doing it. Without saying it in so many words, I knew it was because he didn't want to share the limelight with the others. I lost my temper to his face explaining this was about charity not him and wasn't rugby a team game anyway? But he stood his ground because he knew he was hot property and intended to very much keep it that way.

With my head in my hands and the frustration rising to furious levels you don't want to reach when coming up against an angry woman, I sought a compromise. I was beginning though to see what hard work he was and how frustrating he was going to be to many others. We finally agreed that one picture would be of him alone and one would be taken with the rest of the team, but of course the picture the press all used in the end was the one of just Danny.

Which to him proved his point. And I suppose it did.

My frustrations seemed to be shared with the manager I had set him up with though.

Stuart Higgins kept saying to me during this time "This is a nightmare, a complete nightmare. I have stories about him coming at me all the time about what he has been up to and I'm spending all hours firefighting rather than just promoting him."

I knew that Danny had a touch of growing up to do but I felt protective of him. There were stories of him going to nightclubs before games, of black eyes after nights out. He was a troubled genius but then

I suppose they all are. Injuries started to arrive and when in May 2008 I watched an awful one happen to him, as I was actually at the game, where he had fractured his ankle, it was like it had happened to my brother. I felt physically sick. He was getting no luck and I felt incredibly frustrated for him, but as ever he didn't help himself by starting to have fights with his fellow team mates on the training ground. In 2010 he had moved on from Wasps and was in danger of becoming a superstar that clubs were reluctant to take on as his bad behaviour continued, with him swearing on TV and getting papped leaving nightclubs again and again in the early hours.

But I was really getting into Rugby at this time. So, I will digress slightly before I return to the chapters central story. I happened to be in Selfridges one day with Joy Desmond looking at the perfume and opposite us was a guy whom I recognised instantly. It was Dan Carter, the greatest player in the world at that time and who was also captain of New Zealand the best and most feared team in International Rugby.

He came over to talk to us at the counter and after some small talk I said to the great one in my usual shy and retiring way:

"I work on TV and we have a party tonight to celebrate the second series of my show, ITV at the Movies. All the heads will be there plus lots of press, why don't you come along?"

I gave him the address of the party and waltzed away out of Selfridges and onto Oxford Street. I must confess I then forgot all about it as I got ready to go to Fulham for the night's entertainment. About an hour into the event, a very troubled bouncer came rushing over, just about finding me as it was packed out that night with a huge media crowd in attendance.

"You need to come with me now Lizzie there is an issue at the door" he said.

I battled through the masses and there he was by the entrance, Mr Dan Carter, but not on the guest list apparently. That couldn't possibly have been anything to do with me forgetting to put him on there in the first place because I had had a few drinks before I arrived that night. It must have been an administration error. Probably.

"Hey Lizzie can I come in?" said the best rugby player in the world, very politely I have to say. His parents had bought him up well.

I'm sure I replied "Yes" but it may have been "yeehhahhsss…hic" as I had had even more to drink by that point in the evening. Well it was my party it would have been rude not to darlings.

The head bouncer just looked at me in total and utter amazement, followed in unison by everyone of his team of bouncers. He then came out with the world famous Shakespearian phrase:

"Are you for fucking real Lizzie?!"

I waved him away in that spoilt princess diva way and as I turned on my diva heels and started to walk back to the group I was with, I thought "One more guest won't matter, what a jobsworth, it's a total fuss about nothing."

Suddenly there was a huge commotion behind me and a massive intake of breath from every one of the guests. That must have been the fuss about nothing. I stopped and turned around and to my total jaw-dropping astonishment there wasn't just one rugby player coming in, Dan was leading every single member of the All Blacks rugby squad into the party. And these were not just men darlings, these were UBER men.

I told you it was a fuss about nothing.

They were just simply huge. Massive. Mesmerizing. Massively Mesmerizing. Ladies, type 'New Zealand Haka' into Google, sit down with a glass of white wine and once you have watched that clip once, pour another glass and invite your friends over to watch it too. That will cheer up any bad day for you trust me darlings. Pause it a few times too so you can study them properly.

The mind boggles on the scene outside though before they came in.

Like possibly Dan approaching the bouncers, getting turned away but standing his ground and shouting "I'm coming in anyway mate!"

The bouncer then growls at him:

"Oh yeah? You and whose army?"

"Err this one sunshine" as 20 All Blacks walk around the corner to line up behind him.

Or imagine if some young kid had tried to queue jump that night as the All Blacks waited patiently in line?

Or fancy being the actual bouncer who stood there and refused entry to them? That is the winner of the 'Bouncer of the year' award right there.

"I don't care if you are the fucking All Blacks squad mate your names aren't on the guest list so you ain't coming in."

As for Danny Cipriani, in the years 2008 to 2010 we became platonically close, so much so that on the day after Jason had sped away, he text me saying he thought something was wrong and was I ok? I pretended I was fine, as I would do for a while to everyone, but he didn't believe me and as soon as the story broke properly a month or so after, he was immediately messaging me again asking to meet up.

We arranged to meet for a drink at Magnums, a wine bar in Richmond, and I can't say at that stage I was either nervous or excited about seeing him, I just needed a friend so I went along. We had a lovely evening together though and at the end he asked me if I could drop him to his car which was parked on Richmond Green. So off we went, it wasn't far away.

Having just parked up, suddenly, and with no one taking the lead, we kissed in the car. And we didn't stop for the best part of two hours. It was the greatest kiss of all time. It was the kiss that Shakespeare wrote about in Romeo and Juliet 500 years earlier, though he probably didn't expect it would happen where it did.

"Romeo, Romeo wherefore art thou Romeo?"

"On a bit of grass just off the high street in Richmond oh great Bard, but that doesn't matter to us."

And at that moment nothing did.

Let me say it again for the effect it deserves. It was the greatest kiss of all time. I remember thinking I had never ever been kissed like that in my entire life, and in that first initial moment, in the first 20 seconds, I realised what I had been missing all those years. The windows steamed up and stayed like that the whole time. In-between kissing, the way he stared at me was simply breath-taking, his eyes told me he wanted me and the feeling that gave me sent such passion through my body that at times he had me on the verge of fainting.

It wasn't just the thought of someone wanting me again. It wasn't just because I may have been caught in a weak moment because it was only a month since I had split with my husband. If that kiss had happened at any stage in my entire life I would have felt the same way. Sure, my God I needed it, but that wasn't all. I felt excited again, I felt like a woman again and I felt desired again. I hadn't had that feeling for years.

On the way home, I could hear the texts coming through and when I read them I felt the same way as he did.

"It was magical, I am still tingling now."

"God that was amazing do you feel the same?"

"Can't you come back, I just don't want this evening to ever end, ever."

It brought sparks back into my life. Those butterfly feelings you get as they float and fly around your body. It lit something in me which had been lying still for years and maybe had been actually dormant for the whole of my entire life so far.

The following night I was again in Wimbledon and my friends were becoming worried about me. They had a point, I was worried about me too, but I knew something they didn't. I remained silent about the previous night's events and spent most of those few hours with them just checking my phone for his text which I knew must be coming.

Checking, checking, checking.

And then it arrived. Opening that text was like the feeling you had when you opened your exam results. I was excited yet utterly petrified. The message simply said *"He had to see me right now,*

23

where was I?" Not expecting me to reply *"5 minutes away."* I was 'in his manor' he told me which meant, according to him and his law of the jungle, I couldn't refuse his request.

Fair enough, who was I to turn down Tarzan.

He sent me his address, though bizarrely telling me at the same time to *"Gently tap on the door"* when I arrived and *"be a bit quiet"* when I pulled up outside.

I soon found out why. He still lived at home with his mum.

Now I saw this right away as endearing and if truth be told what did I really expect? He was still just in his early 20's after all. I was double his age. I was in my forties, but it didn't matter at all to me. Nothing did, ever, when it related to him.

His mums house was a lovely semi down a normal road and when I approached the door it immediately opened before I could knock on it. A bit like the door at Number 10 always opens for the Prime Minister and you never see the person inside actually doing it. Can you imagine if it didn't open? The PM would then bang on the door repeatedly, look through the window to see if anyone was there before remembering the spare key was hidden under the doormat all along.

In my case, the invisible door-opener was Danny. As I entered the porch to his mum's house he put his finger to his lips as if to say shut up Lizzie, which in fairness often happens to me readers but not usually on the first minute of a date. But it became clear why when he started to tiptoe in a very exaggerated slow-motion way past the front room, the door of which had been firmly closed.

So, there I was behind him, copying his exaggerated tiptoeing moves with my stilettos still on, which isn't easy let me tell you, when he whispered/mouthed to me "My mums in there" pointing to the room behind the closed door. She wouldn't have been able to hear though as I remember Coronation Street was on loudly in the background. When I passed, I just breathed a silent sigh of relief. This whole thing just reminded me of my teenage years.

Then my James Bond like mission seemed destined to have failed. A man in old fashioned cotton pyjamas, which had frankly seen better days let me tell you, ambled towards me at the bottom of the stairs. Before I could muster an attempt at "Hi, I'm Lizzie" Danny grabbed my arm and manoeuvred me away, whispering "it's ok, it's just the lodger" which I'm not sure did make it ok at all but it didn't matter as the lodger totally ignored me anyway and walked on by.

Thank God he didn't ask for a selfie.

The whole thing was turning into a theatre farce but it just made it even more dramatic, even more exciting, even more dangerous.

The stairs creaked one by one as I went up them which made my heart race even faster, wondering at which exact point Mum Cipriani would come out and see the bum of 42 year old Lizzie Cundy tiptoeing up her stairs towards her son's bedroom for a few hours of unashamed naughty fun. But I made it up to the top without being summoned to explain my MILF-like intentions and into the small room I went, which just about had a double bed squeezed in.

It was massively untidy, a teenager's bedroom that was for sure and the reality really started to hit me.

But, frankly my dear, I didn't give a damn.

This wasn't a mid-life crisis, though, out of context no doubt it would be seen that way. It was a man and a woman wanting each other, simple as that. The setting was irrelevant. We started to kiss and it went on from there.

At this point as I write on a cold rainy November day I am torn between the dilemma of revealing quite naughty things about my relationships in general or to be demure and frankly rise above all of that, as of course demure ladies do. I know you are all now shouting "TELL, TELL, TELL - I've paid good money for this book I want some action!" but I have to say a very polite but firm NO to you my darlings.

I realise we are now becoming friends, and I like that as you are lovely, but we are not close enough just yet. Harsh I know but very fair I feel. So, I shall just hint around the edges instead. My education, which was a school run by nuns, actually installed a sense of decorum in me which you may find totally bewildering after seeing half-naked racy pictures of me online page after Google page, but it's a fact. Therefore, let's invent a phrase which we can refer to as we go through the journey in this book and call it 'the naughty scale'.

That night with Danny was a big 9 out of 10 on the naughty scale.

To gather some perspective on that, a 1 is a cuddle with your onesie on whilst watching Gardeners World on TV and a 10 is having sex in the toilets of The Ivy restaurant with Hagaan Daaz rubbed all over every part of you instead of eating it politely at the table for dessert.

Twenty minutes or so into our naughty 9 rated extravaganza, Danny whispered suddenly "Be quiet," it had to be said, rather loudly, and I thought he was talking to himself for a moment as I rarely made any 'noise' in bed. But then I suddenly realised he was talking to me and the 'noises' were indeed mine. Blimey, that's a turn up for the old books I said to myself as I carried on being noisy, and sodded the shameful consequences of a noisy discovery by Mummy C.

I had been in his room for an hour or so, when the carry on like farce got even more of a farce. Farcegate in fact.

"Danny, Danny" called up his mum from the bottom of the stairs, "do you want your dinner now son?"

"Err, errrrrr, give me 5 minutes" shouted down the now first official new lover I had been with in 23 years. It was the sort of proud moment you would get a certificate for at school and be presented with it at assembly in front of everyone.

When his mum called up to Danny, it was the only time I ever saw him less than fully confident. Slightly humbled and ever so embarrassed he said to me "I will go and make sure she is in the kitchen and you just run out of the door when I give the signal, is that ok?"

And who said romance was dead?

Sure enough, more scared of his mum than scared of me, he went downstairs as I got dressed in Olympic 100 metre speed and waited at the top of those same stairs crouched down in the darkness like a coiled lioness. The Lip gloss Lioness in fact.

He suddenly stuck his head around the kitchen door and 'The Richmond Romeo' gave me a wave. I waved back and blew a kiss for effect.

"What a darling you are Danny" I thought to myself.

And yet he looked frustrated and a tad annoyed with me which was heart-breaking in that cupid arrow moment, until it dawned on me after his 4th wave, which was more of a pointy aggressive jab, it had to be said, that it was actually the coded signal for The Cundetta to leave the house!

I took two stairs at once as I bounded down like Tigger from Winnie the Pooh on a space hopper, running for my life and my dignity. I nodded a nod of familiarity to the cotton pyjama lodger on the way out, who didn't appear to have moved from his spot an hour before and bounded into my car, speeding away like a very satisfied bank robber into the now dark London night.

And how did I react in that moment? How did I feel? I felt bloody amazing that's how I felt.

On went Spandau Ballet's 'Gold' and I sang my heart out all the way home.

I have never felt more alive.

Sing with me ladies:

"These are my salad days slowly being eaten away" I belted out as I thought about my marriage.

"Oh, but I'm proud of you, but I'm proud of you" I shouted out loudly to myself.

"You're indestructible, always believe in coz you are - Gold!" I shouted to myself again in case I didn't hear myself shout the first time.

I didn't call anyone on the way home I didn't need to. I just sang and sang. Gold on repeat.

Despite my new-found belief that life wasn't really that bad anymore, I vowed not to tell anyone right away about Danny. This guy could become one of the biggest rugby stars in the world and I didn't need the attention, the questions or the press finding out. And that wasn't because I felt guilty as my break-up had only been a month or so before. Why should I? Danny had given me confidence that the future may just be ok, not necessarily with him but because I still had some fire inside of me. I liked myself again and even more so when he continued to heap more and more compliments onto me each time we met or texted each other.

However, after that first amazing night, pretty much our whole time on and off together was one continued teen-like experience. He had now been picked for the England Rugby squad and one night he smuggled me into his room in Pennyhill Park where the whole squad was staying. The next morning, I went down to leave and saw all the team and the coaches in reception and so I hid behind a plant pot until they had left, just thinking "Oh my God what am I doing?" at the same time as thinking "oh my God this is so dangerously exciting". We would regularly meet up at hotels, or at his mum's house, with his mum still not knowing, sometimes doing the same routine as on the first night. The lodger seemed to be the only one who knew but he seemed to be in a continual cotton pyjama world of his own. I'm not sure he ever spoke to anyone in the house, let alone me.

But in reality, there were limited places we could go to. I didn't want him at my house, he never came and he never met my children.

Indeed, for the 4 years we were on and off together I don't think he ever met anyone who was close to me. Which summed it up I suppose as the sexually fuelled relationship it was. He did however meet one person though.

My ex-husband.

Jason interviewed him for his Talk Sport show during this period and he didn't know a thing about what had happened. Which I didn't gloat about inwardly at the thought but I did see the utter irony of it. Jason can be quite intimidating but Cipriani was Cipriani, a real rugby man, a man's man, an uber man and he wasn't scared of anyone.

He was happy to go on his show, knowing what he knew.

It was however worryingly turning into love. On my side at least. I could feel it coming but I lived off the excitement our meetings produced, I knew I shouldn't be doing it but I didn't care. One bit.

That was until the problems started which frankly were obviously always going to start.

I was at a Wimbledon tennis event, which Danny happened to be at too with his manager. Stuart Higgins looked at how we were around each other and said to me when we were alone:

"Oh my God you aren't shagging him, are you?"

"Deny, deny, deny" he had himself taught me as I mentioned before, so I did just that.

Denied, denied, stomped my foot in an outraged temper and stated very firmly to him:

"Don't be so ridiculous Stuart, that is outrageous, insulting and I'm very upset you could ever think like that about me."

To which he responded, the bloody smart arse:

"So, you are shagging him then. Well a word of advice, don't let anyone know about this, it's just 8 months in, you don't need the grief of it right now. You really don't."

But grief is what I started to get though regardless. The papers were reporting a lot about him being with other girls and with Kelly Brook especially. This wasn't a normal relationship in that we never ever said we were 'going out' in a boyfriend/girlfriend type of way but there was a feeling certainly on my part, we probably were. But that didn't stop him seeing other girls and his deny, deny, deny and then duck out of the truth was masterful.

I eventually told some friends about us and when I did the reaction was unanimous. They thought I was totally mad. Especially Jay who I had been close to for years and then suddenly became distant with me because of it. They all said the same thing, that he had a bad vibe about him, he was arrogant and he was using me. They said this isn't good for you and you have changed. And for good measure they threw in that he was not bringing out a good side of me, what is the future between you?

I knew all of what they said but still ignored it. It was hard to see the wrong in him ever. I even used my contacts in the press to try and stop stories about him appearing. One I couldn't stop though was in 2013 when a hint of what we were up to finally, after 3 years, appeared in The Sun.

It was my birthday and the traditional birthday texts started to come through. But one was not what I expected.

It was from Dan Wotten the executive editor of The Sun newspaper. My heart sank, any text from The Sun on a Saturday morning was not going to be good news.

"Lizzie we know about you and Danny, we are thinking of running a piece tomorrow on it."

Gulp.

Double gulp.

This was indeed a gulparama moment.

But The Sun themselves had taught me what to do in these exact circumstances.

Deny, deny, deny.

"Oh, Dan, don't be so silly darling, nothing is going on" I confidently tried to reply which was almost impossible as I suddenly just could not breathe.

You could tell he wasn't falling for it. And why would he? He was the best in the business by a country mile and had been for some time.

So, in my utter desperation I called up Danny.

"You need to stop this Lizzie, my God I have a big game tomorrow! I can't take this, it's so unfair, I don't need this grief right now!" he moaned.

Which I suppose summed him up. It was all about him. That's all he was used to, in sport, in relationships, in love. When I replied "What about me then, this will affect me too" he came back with the threat of "Well don't see me then" which I couldn't contemplate at that moment and he probably knew that, so I did try to stop it and stop it at 100 miles an hour deny, deny, deny pace.

But looking back what a fool I was! Of course, Dan Wotten knew it was true. And I regret to this day trying desperately to stop the story appearing as it just made me look ridiculous and they ran the story anyway. Why wouldn't they?

But I was blinded by a love which simply and heartbreakingly did not love me back.

The Sun 17-08-13

'Love-rat Danny Cipriani has been exchanging flirty texts with a 45-year-old divorcee believed to be a friend of his mum.

The 25-year-old rugby star messaged former WAG Lizzie Cundy as his relationship with model Kelly Brook, 33, hit the skids.

Socialite Cundy used to be married to ex-Chelsea footballer Jason Cundy, and is close to another of Kelly's exes, Thomas Evans, 28.

A source said: "Danny and Lizzie have sent flirtatious messages to each other for a long time. She's old enough to be his mother so it's clear nothing physical would happen, it was all a bit of harmless fun."

Lizzie insisted she did not text Sale Sharks star Danny while he was with Kelly.

His spokesman said Lizzie was advising him on the media fallout of his split.'

Again and again, I believed everything he said to me even though he was still being described as a serial cheat in the papers. When I knew he had definitely gone off with someone else, and more often than not with Kelly Brook, I stopped seeing him but then went back when he told me it was over with whichever girl it was then over with. Like the complete love fool that I was, I thought the sun shone everywhere on him and up him.

We used to row whenever I saw a story in a paper about his antics, even once when I saw a picture of him on a fairground ride with a girl, but he would deny it every time. Despite hard photo evidence he would deny it. As I kept wanting to believe him, I therefore did believe him. But I cried many nights over my suspicions and each time I broke it off or indeed went back to him it was tough as my heart never ever wanted to leave.

But above all else, I didn't want to be his mistress. I couldn't do that to myself or especially to the girl he may have been seeing. Even to this day I don't know how he felt about me, deep down, but in the end I broke away properly as there comes a time when you have to go into rehab for a drug and in my case that is what he was to me. I was his heroine I'm sure for brief moments in time but he was my heroin and I had to stop taking it.

I did love him though. Deeply.

Cheeky Blagger

"She is very much misunderstood by the public, but she has to some degree brought that upon herself. She is fun, she has such a kind soul, but she is as daft as a brush. She is very sensitive, very fragile and we have grown up together with her always being like that. She is true to who she is, she has never been a 'conservative' person. Lizzie was the ring leader when we were teenagers and I was the follower, she would just push her way to the front of a queue and blag her way into anything. She was cheeky and knew how to humour anyone, that together with the very flirtatious nature she has, got her accepted in that celebrity world.

She just likes people and is always very complimentary to them.

Love finds you when you are ready and I think she needs to love herself first before she finds it.

You have to see beyond the glitter, everyone she meets adores her, my mum adores her, everyone's mum adores her. She can be a tiny bit irresponsible but that is her playful character. If you said you can't wear ripped jeans anymore she would just say why and don't tell me what to wear. I've seen both boys grow up and they have become great men, developed into wonderful people. The 3 of them hang out together and have fun together. She got them through that very painful period after Jason by herself. I always got on with Jason funnily enough, but he was very challenging and the break-up was long and painful.

She was always more comfortable in the celebrity surroundings than I, she found it very natural. But she is like that to all people, she could walk into her local pub in the country and she would know all their names. She was never starstruck back then, she just sees everyone as people.

I've known her at her happiest and I've known her in her darkest period and she never has sought revenge, she believes in Karma and is too kind-hearted to want that anyway."

Jay King (formerly Jay Gordon) - friend of Lizzie's since 1986

The divorce from Jason finally came through in late 2012. Whilst I was in many ways relieved it was over, it had paid a heavy price on both my emotions and my finances. He had started the proceedings some time before and as he launched first against me, he was able to say he was divorcing me on the grounds of my 'unreasonable behaviour'. Which was frankly complete and utter nonsense.

Those two words, 'unreasonable behaviour' immediately bring up the picture in most people's minds that I had cheated on him. Which I never did. The simple fact is he said I was being 'unreasonable' towards him due to my lack of 'attention' to his ego presumably, which as I touched on in the opening chapter, happened, if indeed it did happen, because of my TV work.

Nothing more to say. No story.

The public's perception of an ex-wife of a premier league footballer is there must be plenty of money flying round. I understand that, but in my case he had retired some years before and the plain truth was I was earning more money than he was when we split. Which I did in the last few years of marriage to keep the family in the lifestyle they had been accustomed to. Now that was being claimed as 'unreasonable' because I should have been at home being 'reasonable' to my husband. Well he didn't think it was unreasonable before August 2010 when I was bringing that money in and he was, in part, spending it.

And because I was working that hard, the divorce agreement ended up with me having to pay him alimony and him paying me nothing. So, I had to keep working hard to fund someone who complained that me working hard was unreasonable when we were married, but now because he wanted money, even though we had split up 2 years before, it was suddenly reasonable that I should continue to work as hard as I did.

So, therefore, I was being unreasonably reasonable.

I know what you are thinking and I agree. It doesn't and never will make any sense to me either.

I wanted to work but now I HAD to work. There is a difference. There was not much money in the pot and it would be down to me to get my boys through their teenage years.

Workwise, I only knew how to be me. I didn't have a special skill in anything or special training. I wasn't a doctor, I wasn't selling an idea. I could only sell me. And not in that way you naughty reader, though I have been offered 'any money I like' by a very rich sports owner to sleep with him, which I have declined to do on many occasions.

Selling me was therefore not a bad idea for a career. I'm an expert on me. My mastermind subject would be me, I'm that much of an expert.

So, when those pictures come up on Google of Lizzie Cundy, please understand darlings I never really did anything like that for my own self-promotion, I did it to earn a living. Which I very much needed to do and in fact still do. A premiership football players wealth seemed to have passed me by somewhere. I had to pay the rent.

I could earn money in a number of ways. Through TV work, through writing columns for papers/magazines and through radio. And I could earn it by bringing PR to someone's launch or event by coming along and getting the press to photo me doing so. It would then appear in the papers and bring attention to those that had paid me. And I could also get paid from clothes companies to wear their things when I was getting 'papped'.

And I knew I would be good at that because I suppose in some ways I am an attention seeker. I like to make people laugh and be in the centre of things.

After the marriage break I made a conscious decision that in order to be as successful as I could be, I would become more risqué when I went out and more daring. There would be an element of suspicion that I did that to show Jason 'what he was missing' but I don't believe I ever did that consciously, though fair enough could have done it subconsciously.

The racy clothes I wore would make me appear to most people I suppose a *man-eater* but I simply am not. I hope when you read the rest of the book you will come to that conclusion too. And I guess now looking back I may have been dressing that way to look younger when in fact it may have had the reverse effect.

I have never gone searching for the paparazzi ever when I've been out with just friends. I think celebrity and fame are addictive but I would never try and engineer that. My good friend Patsy Kensit said to me once that it is impossible to get off that addiction, but for me fame means money and I'm a working mum. Therefore I need both.

The realisation that a picture could drive huge press interest first really came to me in the Christmas of 2010 when I had just split with Jason. I was photographed on the beach on holiday in a white bikini and got loads of coverage. I remember thinking "Blimey, is that all it takes?"

In the years following 2010, there was one 'infamous' night in particular when I was photographed wearing a totally see-through dress with red underwear underneath. But it was matching darlings, so I had some decorum. Put the words Lizzy Cundy into Google now, look at *images* and you will see that picture there. I have also put it into the photos section in this book too for dramatic effect.

What happened on that particular night was some friends had a restaurant opening and the owners needed press. Nothing unusual there. As is normally the case I was paid to get promotion for that opening but I could tell here that we needed a big impact as the owners were panicking. It had been arranged at the last minute and I had only received the call that very morning.

I sat and thought, what would get the most press? The most attention? I went to the boot of my car to find the answer. No not to see if Mickey Rourke was still in there so I could bring him, but instead to find a dress. One of life's greatest facts is the boot of a car is a good place to keep loads of things a lady may need. In my case, that was clothes to wear at any event at the last minute. I found the dress I needed which I had been given by a fashion designer some weeks before, but I did stop for a second and think - hang on you have a red bra and knickers on underneath, is this really going to be good for you? And who knows if it has been good for me generally or not but it got the desired effect for those paying me that night especially as the pictures went everywhere with details about the restaurant opening the next day.

When I am dressed a little inappropriately, I don't leave the house like that. I stop off at this hotel I know in London, get changed, tip off the paps and make my way to the opening. After the work is over I will do the same thing in reverse and drive home walking into the house in normal clothes as I don't want my boys to see me like that in person.

The boys reaction to all this has been a problem, I cannot deny that. Whilst I tried to always walk in nicely dressed, it's a tricky one to hide when your pictures are online or in the papers the next day.

And right up until Shirley Valentine in 2018, I have carried on the same trick. Last year I had a client who was a barber shop owner and we had planned for some celebs to come to his opening but they decided at the last minute not to show up, which I think is so unprofessional. The owners were obviously upset and desperate for the promotion they were after, so I sat there and thought how can we still get coverage? The only answer was for my top to come off and for me to pretend to cut hair in my bra. No logic in it I know but it worked. As it happened I had an Ann Summers bra on so I got a bonus as my great friend, Jacqui Gold, the boss of Ann Summers, rang me after and sent me one in every colour.

I have been offered to go further with things like Playboy but have never and would never do that.

I have to keep being a 'celebrity' as that is my job. I'm not denying 'God what a job' sometimes, but it is bloody hard work and you take a lot of knocks in the process. But I am comfortable in that life because my whole life has been in that world right from a very early age.

Now when you normally read the part in a book where the childhood is revealed, you probably skip it like I do and get to the good parts about a third of the way in. I appreciate I'm biased here but not only would it be really useful if you didn't get bored right now darlings as it sets the scene for my start in a celebrity life, but I'm also about to reveal my time spent with George Michael, Madonna, Prince and many major other stars of the 80's.

I don't want you to miss out. I'm nice like that.

It was 1983, I was 14 and I had skived off school yet again. Why? Because it was a maths lesson and me and the mighty Pythagoras were not bonding in any way and frankly unlikely to ever it has to be said. I was sat in Covent Garden with a fellow friend in skiving teenage solidarity, when this long blond haired man with an outrageously loud leopard print jacket on walks past us, double takes then returns back to where we were sitting to talk to us.

"Are you a model sweetheart?" he asked me. "If not you should be as you are totally gorgeous" and for maximum effect he added "and if you had a modelling card you could come into my club for free."

I had absolutely no idea who he was. I just giggled. But Mr Leopard print jacket was none other than Peter Stringfellow the original King of clubs. Now, at this point you may be thinking sleazebag (him, not me) and here we go an older man hitting on a younger girl, but it was nothing of the sort in his case. He was a really nice guy with such a lovely smile, he simply loved being around attractive ladies. Which may make him a sleazebag in society's definition, but he wasn't and you will have to take my word on that as he has sadly passed away. He was a total gentleman on that first meeting and in fact was in all my subsequent time spent with him over the years.

Which were many.

"Go see this lady and tell him Peter sent you honey" he said giving me details of a model agency he knew.

So, I rang this lady called Stella from the phone box and she said you must come in now which is what I did. It was that or more maths and that wasn't a tricky decision for a 14 year old to make. When I arrived I was signed up on the spot and that not only meant a Stringfellow's membership but also I received an instant offer of a modelling job there and then for a bridal shoot happening later that day.

Me being me and having fairly good morals (honestly) I made the potentially fatal mistake of telling the truth. I mentioned to a lady working there, Lulu, that I was 14, born in May 1968 and would this be a problem? Which of course it obviously would be.

But she just laughed it off, telling me that in a modelling career I had to remember two things. Lie about my age and always have matching nail varnish. So, the 14 year old then immediately proclaimed she had got her real age wrong the first time, so sorry, very careless of her and that she was in fact really 18.

"Excellent"said the excellent Lulu, "you are hired."

Lie, lie, lie was her mantra, so for the next 3 years that's what I did. In fact, right up until the day before my 50th birthday I continued to lie about my real age.

The mid 80's for me was an outrageous period. It was a wild period. It was a think on your feet fast time of life, you had to be street smart to survive it and I was definitely that. I had to grow up quickly at home as many times from an early age I was left alone when mum and dad went out. Indeed, when my parents were actually at home I would meet celebrity after celebrity because my father was Art Director for 'Saatchi and Saatchi' the world famous advertising agency and my mum was boss of Jaeger the fashion brand. My father had in fact planned the whole conservative party general election advertising campaign in 1979 which has been credited as the main reason for getting Margaret Thatcher elected after years of a labour government. He was very influential in London society.

He also hung out with photographers and they were around the house all the time especially David Bailey and Duffy, who has now become uber famous because he was the photographer who did Bowie's world famous and iconic Aladdin Sane album cover.

So, I was now a model and because of my upbringing I felt totally at ease in that world. I wanted Stringfellow's access and I wanted money. I got both. It wasn't the attention really at all for me then, it was just the fun of it. I enjoyed the camaraderie, the mucking around. The money was good but I saved pretty much every bit of it. It could have been a life of sleaze but for me it wasn't. I never slept with anyone during those early years and I never took any drugs. But because of my outgoing personality, I just seemed to go from one crazy adventure to another right, through every A-list music star you could think of from the mid 1980's. I was simply great at blagging my way into anything. World class blagger was Lizzie Miller, as I was known then of course. A blagger is defined as someone 'who gets what they want in a clever way' and that was me I suppose. I would

Above: Writing the scandal for my book on the beach.

Above: Modelling in South Africa for a Hello! mag shot.

Left: Mickey Rourke - the infamous car night!

Below: With Mickey Rourke and Sheryl Howard.

Above: Acting the idiot! With my good school mates Nikki Ferguson and Roxy Medina (who all the boys loved) and she went off with my first boyfriend /crush Martin Leciester Grey! I was heartbroken!! First taste of a boy being disloyal... story of my life!

Nikki sadly killed herself. We both loved drama, dancing and acting silly.

Left: The grey haired lady is PJ Powers who sung the national anthem to the World Cup opening, good chums with Nelson Mandela and me. The guy far right, the Simon Cowell of South Africa, is Eric Way and the girl on the far left is the South African WAG Sonia Booth.

Below: Me with my first born Josh.

Right: Kissing the World Cup in SA

Below: Fellow South African WAG shoot for OK! mag... but everyone just wanted to know about the English WAGs!

Above: Loving my bikinis!!! Poser!!

Above: World Cup, didn't stop working. Soweto charity days with Eric Way... where are the WAGs? Fabio wouldn't let them out!!!

Left: On family holiday with Josh in Sardinia.

Right: My manager and my great friend Vickie White... on another mission.

Left: With the Bodyguard National Television Awards winner Richard Madden and my pal Becky Vardy.

Right: Wanted to be a punk in supermodel competition final.

Below: Children orphanage in Johannesburg with fellow South African WAG Sonia Booth.

Left: Me and my besties Joy Desmond and Sian Welby.

Below: Taking on Hollywood! On TV back home from Hollywood.

Above: At Simon's summer party; Lauren Silverman and me always turn up in the same colour.

Above: Outside Bruno's off to Simon's party.

Right: Boys are best friends. First day of school for my James.

Below: Me and Meghan Markle. The last interview before she met Harry.

Above: Me over 6 month preggers with Josh, still modelling trying to hide the bump with my old model chum Jay Gordon.

Right: Modelling pic that got me the Bond movie.

Below: On the James Bond set for the film Goldeneye.

Above: Barbados modelling shot.

Above: Little Lizzie Miller. My dad always said I had mischief in my eyes!

Left: My dear friend Paul Young. one of my many Showbiz guests.

Below: My new TV show WAGs World launched with this poster.

Right: Good friend Meg Mathew's, Noal Gallaghers ex. We both have the same interests and support animal charities.

Below: My night out with Liza Minnelli.

Above: Once a Cundy always a Cundy. A rare picture of me in flats!

Right: My ITV This Morning show exclusive interview with Simon Cowell.

Below: Pic of my boys playing tennis with my bestie Paul Cavliar and our friend west end superstar Elaine Paige in Barbados.

Left: Having fun in town with my besties!

Below: My dear friends Lisa Harris, skin specialist to the stars, and lovely This Morning host Ruth Langsford having a girlie catchup.

Above: On the set of the ITV summer show 'Our Shirley Valentine Summer.'

blag my way into everything and people seemed to warm to me. I couldn't care who they were, or how famous they were I just talked my way into everything.

I was carefree, the world was ahead of me and nothing could stop me.

It was early on in my modelling career that I first met the now highly controversial figure, Philip Green. He didn't own Top Shop then but he had a brand, the Jean Genie and I had been asked to go for a casting in a total dump of a warehouse in Shepherds Bush. Skiving off again, I went through the usual "How old are you?" "I'm 18 of course" routine and then towards the end of the day, with me getting panicky as I had to make it home before my dad got in from work, someone said right whoever had the best bum will get through to the shoot. Just as I'm pushing my bum out as far as I could to impress, this voice appears from nowhere and bellows "I will decide who has the best bum!"

Standing there as bottom expert and bum supremo was Phillip Green himself.

I got the gig, feeling a bit bad for *Miss Tiny Arse* next to me but those are the breaks honey. I went through the "How old are you? "I'm 18" routine again but this time with Phillip himself, and walked away with a new photoshoot in the diary.

On the day of the shoot itself, ok, ok, yes I skived, ok, ok, yes I lied that I skived to the school, it was just one laugh after another. This was the first shoot of their's, there were more being lined up for trade shows in Birmingham but first things first was London where we all just couldn't stop laughing and larking about.

In walks Philip Green to the backstage area just as I had finished my hair and make-up and he shouts "For fucks sake, who is making all that noise I've totally had enough!" When I meekly admitted it was me, mainly because everyone had actually pointed at me, he simply said and without any hint of it being a joke:

"No more talking. You lady are sacked. You are gone, go."

I stopped laughing and larking about. As I shamefully walked out of the room he gave me the final reminder "I'm sick of your voice, go!" I shut the door and went out into the pissing it down with rain London day and got the number 37 bus back to Richmond.

When I got home my mum could not believe I was sacked. I was ashamed. I just felt I had let Lulu at the agency and everyone down. That didn't placate my mum, she was furious.

And my mum readers is someone you don't want to make furious. She is very posh, she speaks like the queen but she is also very, very protective and has gotten me out of many scrapes in my time. As all mothers I'm sure, she sees no wrong in me and that is probably where I picked up my trait of seeing no wrong in men.

But she was also hugely influential, none more so than her guidance on the important of lip gloss in the daily life of a lady. I remember from an early age watching her put her make-up on before she ever went out and her reminding me to never leave the house without lip gloss on.

"You never know who you will meet darling" was her mantra and I have lived by that my whole life. I got most of my 'training' on social skills from her.

That evening the phone rang at home. It was Phillip Green. He wanted to speak to me but instead my mum took the phone call.

Green against Gloria. Good luck Phil you are going to need it darling.

Phillip - "Ah, Mrs Miller, it's Phillip Green here owner of Jean Genie. Look I'm sorry about today's events which you have probably heard about, it had been a bad day and I simply lost my temper. I apologise. I just wanted to say Lizzie is of course not fired and we very much hope to see her back at work again tomorrow."

Gloria - "Mr Greeeeeen, you are nothing more than a pompous bullying scoundrel and Elizabeth is not returning to work for you tomorrow or indeed ever again. She is too good for your company and you in particular so please, Sir, do not call this number ever again. Good day to you" and banged the phone down on the soon to be multi billionaire.

Gloria 1 Green 0.

Some years later, Simon Cowell relayed that story to Phillip on a night out on holiday with me and the group I was with, teasing him relentlessly for hours which made me laugh out loud again and again. I met Phillip quite a few times after at various charity events over the years and I forgave him long ago, but my mother never ever did.

I have known Simon for a long time but our first meeting was quite something. I was eating with Jay at my favourite Italian restaurant, Cipriani's in Mayfair, discussing the usual nonsense best friends talk about, when she happened to notice that Simon Cowell was sat at his usual favourite table, which I discovered later was always available for him in case he turned up. It must have been about 16 years ago as he was doing Pop Idol at the time, the show which would eventually lead onto X Factor.

In Cipriani's there is a secret toilet that only the trusted powerful customers or the total blagger's (e.g. me) knew existed and as I needed to go to the toilet desperately at the end of our meal, I headed to the secret section so I didn't have to queue. I assumed I was the only part of this exclusive club there that night so I left the door unlocked. Or I may have been tipsy and forgotten to lock it. Or I never lock the door. You can decide darlings which version suits the story better.

A minute or so later, into the toilet walks Simon. Apparently, he too was part of the secret society - though on the powerful side of the membership no doubt, presumably not having to blag his way into joining in the first place. In fairness it may have actually been his toilet.

So, there I was facing the most important person in UK TV, possibly World TV, sat firmly on the loo seat with my skirt down by my ankles trying to look demure. Now I ask you readers, what do you do in these circumstances? They didn't teach you this at school, or maybe they did and I missed it when I was in Stringfellows. Who says what? Who does what in the opening act of monumental embarrassment on both sides?

What were my options??

Get up coolly, flick my hair about a bit, shuffle over to him with my knickers around my ankles and shake his hand? If so, should I call him Si, Simon, Simmo or just plain Sir?

Casually try and move the large plant by the toilet to just in front of me, hoping he hadn't seen me yet?

Tell him I was just warming the seat up for him and it was all now part of the Cipriani's VIP service?

Start chatting about make-up with him, like you do with your friends when you go into a nightclub toilet together and then move onto gossiping about all the other customers upstairs?

Make out I thought he was the toilet attendant, tell him that the soap and loo roll needed topping up and that he better be quick about it if he wanted his £1 tip!

The stand-off was thankfully suddenly broken:

"Don't I know you?" said the powerful one.

"Not sure, but I know you" said the blagger.

And that was that. He turned around and shut the door, I like to think temporarily guarding it outside for me as I jumped off the seat, pulled everything up and washed my hands with the sheer terror of the moment now sweeping over me.

"Shit, bollocks, shit, damn, shit, shit, bollocks, damn" I whispered to no one at all, as once again in my life I looked into the mirror and gave myself the well-rehearsed Lizzie rallying cry:

"Come on Cunders, you can do this!"

Fresh lip gloss was quickly applied before I took a huge deep breath and opened the door. There he was. Mr Pop Idol. But this time I had all my clothes on which, call me old-fashioned, I always feel is important when meeting someone for the very first time.

"Please let me get you a drink it's the least I can do, come and join us" he gestured upstairs to me very nobly it had to be said.

"Ah that's so sweet darling" I replied, hugging him hello at the same time for maximum Cunders effect. But being the spanner I am, as my arms went around him I caught my watch strap on his jumper. I could see as I peered down his back that the thread was going to unravel if I moved my arm too far.

"Shit, bollocks, shit, damn, shit, shit, bollocks, damn" I whispered again to no one at all and thinking fast, I decided the best course of action was just to carry on cuddling him.

He must have thought I was the friendliest lady he had ever met as we were now attached outside the loo in an endless hug fest. I had the option of either taking loads of his jumper away if I yanked the thread off too quickly, or going into the secret toilet again with him. But it may have been seen as a tad stalkerish and presumptuous that I would want him to share the toilet experience yet again with me, but the other way around this time.

When in doubt I feel the answer readers is always to yank. Which probably makes me a yanker but I didn't care as in that moment it worked. I didn't look to see how big the hole I had made was because I tottered as fast as I could to his table with the hope of pouring a large vodka down my throat quickly to overcome the sheer emotion of the last ten minutes.

And for good measure I then had another.

Taking it all in as best I could, I sat there for an hour or so with them all. But it was in that hour I witnessed, as I would see hundreds of times more over the years following, his power and majesty as celebrity after celebrity came over to pay homage to him. It was simply incredible to watch.

After Cipriani's, we have met in passing on holidays over the years and I have interviewed him numerous times on TV, always concluding the same thing. This man has a kindness inside him that is rarely seen in a human, he is generous not only with his influence but also his time and he treats everyone the same no matter who they are. He isn't arrogant about the power he has, he simply has real power the power to move a room with just a stare, he doesn't have to shout about it and he never does.

Cipriani's started a friendship with him that has been unbroken ever since. Which is either because we get on and have things in common or because once you have seen a lady on the toilet, you have a bond for life.

During the early period of my modelling career I kept the whole thing secret from my father but I was caught out when he happened to answer the phone one day from the modelling agency about a job. He wasn't happy. To say the very least.

My father, Derek Miller, was extremely strict but was a very very hard worker and he installed that ethic in me which I still have to this day. My childhood days were incredibly tough at times though and when he wasn't happy you would know about it. And I often did.

Unfortunately, him picking up the phone that day was about a job for me to be in the video for Curiosity Killed the Cat, the 1980's pop group, and when you have just turned 15, your life is over when you are banned from hanging out with Ben Voltaire their lead singer. Use your brain, life is too short was his constant message to me but I wasn't giving up modelling, so I drip fed occasional jobs I was going on to him, but didn't tell him anything when the photo shoot was just too exciting not to attend. Mum would always cover for me and I only really got acceptance of some sort for that whole period from him was when he told me there were great shots in my modelling book, which I had put together without him. In view of the fact he knew Bailey and Duffy he could have helped me out massively with it, but never did.

I often skived during these years. I wanted to and I had to. I managed to fool the school time and time again by forging my mums handwriting, and when that started to become too obvious I forged my father's instead. The standard line I always used was a sore throat, which trust me you would be surprised how often you can get away with. So, the school never really knew the extent of the work I was doing as the money rolled in. The standard job in the 1980's paid at least £1,000, sometimes £2,000, and I topped it up by doing another business on the side which is when I would forge friends *sick* letters for them. Forgery is a form of art readers, and I was a Picasso for years! The money under my bed kept rising and rising as demand for my services spread.

I went to a convent school nearby where we lived and it was strict. That was the definition when we went in at 9am. By 11am it was stricter, by 1pm it was akin to torture and by 2.30pm the discipline they dished out was probably illegal. God help you if you talked about boys or thought about boys, that was until one day some builders turned up and it was as near as we got to a St. Trinian's revolt. The whole school pressed their faces to the windows in the pursuit of glimpsing men doing, well, anything really.

I was the class joker, the disruptor in chief and everyone would dare me to do things. I would get away with it 90% of the time and the other 10% would result in getting hit on the knuckles with a metal ruler and then the nuns encore would be a slipper whacked many times on my bottom. It was legal violence and the Kray nuns were good at it. When I took their brutality and didn't react they would then make me stand on a chair on my own all afternoon as punishment.

I tried to win the nuns around time and time again and sometimes I actually did. My father used to get loads of samples and gifts through his work and I used to bring them into school to either pay the school bullies to not hit me (a gift of Hubba Bubba gum was good at ensuring that) or to the nuns themselves as a peace offering. One day I gave a bottle of perfume to Sister Bernadette aka one of the Kray nuns and very soon I had a deal whereby if I gave all the nuns a bottle, Reggie nun, aka Sister Bernadette, would secretly take my maths test for me. She led up to that by spending a few weeks also doing my maths homework for me.

It took me a few months after I got my modelling card but I eventually made my way into Stringfellow's for the very first time. I had to pick a moment when I was away modelling so my parents wouldn't find out I was in the 1980's London club of clubs. I had met this girl called Jay Gorden at Silverstone for a Grand Prix job where we were both employed to be Grid Girls. This involved the tricky task of walking with the teams flags around and around the pits. She instantly had me creased up laughing and a friendship for life was born as a result. We were both young, both single and wanted to just live the carefree life you wouldn't find in a maths lesson.

As both of us had model memberships she seemed the perfect underage foil for London clubland, so off we went during the break from Silverstone's events and soon found ourselves in the mecca of 1980's clubland, the hallowed west end nightclub called Stringfellows.

Peter Stringfellow ruled that club like a King, which of course he was. He would sit on his throne and hold court like the modern day Lothario he undoubtedly was. Everyone wanted to be invited onto his table and he was just very friendly without a trace of the abuse of power others would take advantage of. He told me on the first night I was there, "Always feel this is your home" and he started to watch out for me in a purely paternal way.

Within the first hour of arriving though, my Stringers journey nearly ended before it had begun. I was in the toilet and this girl came up behind me, pulled my hair, jumped on me and started pummelling the living daylights out of me, shouting "Leave him alone you bitch!" I assumed the bouncers would rush in, throw me out and ban me forever, but instead of bouncers storming the toilet barricades another girl came rushing in and screamed at my attacker to let me off.

"She isn't the one you are after you bitch, she didn't come onto Eddie!"

Welcome to London clubland baby!

Eddie was apparently Eddie Kidd the famous stunt motorcyclist and my attacker was Stacey Smith who eventually married Paul Young but who sadly passed away in the summer of 2018.

One night, Peter ambled over to us and told my friend and I that Prince was in the club and did I want to meet him?

Mmmm, let me think that one through Mr King of Clubs and I will let you know later on.

But to be in the presence of purple royalty came with caveats attached. "Don't look at him, especially when he is eating, he doesn't like it" lectured Peter "and don't talk to him unless he talks to you." Off to his private table we go where he was surrounded by massive bouncers.

He was frankly very tiny, very odd and very quiet.

"This is my friend Lizzie" said Peter, immediately breaking all the rules by looking at Prince and talking to him before he said anything first but I guess as Peter was the King then a mere Prince's rules wouldn't apply to him!

I sat down at his table before anyone said I couldn't. But all I kept doing with Jay was giggling as I couldn't talk and look at him. Prince was with his girlfriend who had the hairspray and shoulder pads look of the 1980's to perfection and as I was allowed to look at her (with my right eye, the left one being closed in a squint as it would have been looking at Prince), I remember thinking "My God I just have to look like her." When Prince did talk it was in a soft monotone which was barely audible and he usually just nodded when anyone said anything back to him. I spent most of the time looking down at my heels as I was petrified I would look up and see him scoffing his fish finger sandwich at that very moment.

Even though he was, I have to say, pretty damn sexy, we left after half an hour or so as we had frankly better shenanigans to get up to. Like mucking around and drinking.

On most evenings I was there I would arrive before the club opened to get my homework done. No, not by me darlings, but by the bouncers who would do it for me. One of them, Steve, was an absolute genius at maths and by torchlight he would regularly quickly do that for me as I put my make-up on in the toilet.

I wasn't club loyal though to my utter shame, and I started to cheat on Stringers by going across town to a club called Browns, run by Jake Panayiotou. It was there I met every 80's pop star you could ever think of. To name-drop a few, I hung out with Whitney Houston, Bobby Brown, Duran Duran and George Michael. I just always seemed to hit it off with the stars. They liked me I suppose because I was funny and cheeky and I didn't treat them any differently to how I treated my other friends.

No one ever asked my age when I went to Browns because I had the knack of just blagging my way into anything and everything, so they never got an opportunity to. I can't remember if this was a blag or through an actual invite, but I even went back to George Michael's house one night in North London for a party with a group of people.

Yep I am at George Michael's house at the height of his worldwide WHAM fame! But all I kept thinking was 'shit' I haven't done my homework yet. And then when that thought left me it was replaced by shit I had to get the last bus home or I would be in big trouble. My worries were not helped by having to continually fend off the marauding hands of George's bodyguard.

I never once saw Andrew Ridgeley out with George despite their fame together as Wham. I became friends with Andrew recently and spent a wonderful afternoon with him and Simon Le Bon at the England v Ireland 5 nations game. Andrew is one of the of the most stylish men you will ever meet. He turned up at the pub we had arranged to meet at beforehand outside Twickenham looking like Shirley Bassey with a gigantic fur hat on, matching fur coat with a pristine suit underneath.

The hat especially helped to disguise who he was, but when anyone did recognise him he was extremely polite and gracious. He took the piss-taking given to him at half time from the comedian in our hospitality area in great spirit, and was not at all like the media image that is portrayed of him. Simon, Andrew and I huddled together in a 1980s threesome and I have to say darlings, there have been worse moments in my life. Simon and Andrew deep down are just two normal people without any airs and graces and that was evident when we went on a huge pub crawl after the game with Lawrence Dallaglio and his rugby friends. It basically involved drinking 15 pints of lager and singing 'Sweet Charity' on repeat in every pub we could find, and I was therefore always going to be quite good at it.

To complete my tales of 1980's megastar hob-knobbing, I was on a modelling job one day when this guy told me he ran Wembley and did I want to meet Madonna on her 'Who's that Girl' tour? Now this man was obviously trying it on but I put that to one side in my pursuit of the material girl and a few days later found myself in the VIP car park at Wembley Stadium in my friend Wanda's clapped out old Fiat parking up next to a few Bentleys, 8 Range Rovers and a Rolls Royce. Being the VIP I now obviously was, I sat in the same exclusive section watching the concert as George Michael, the Pet Shop Boys and Boy George. There probably were other stars there but all I can recall now is George dancing and miming to all the Madonna songs the whole way through.

When the show ended, Mr Wembley creep came over and asked Wanda and I if we wanted to talk to Madonna as "You know only the special people could meet her honey." I have to say I was in a bit of dilemma if I should go into the depths of Wembley's bottom or not as I was overdue on my maths homework and didn't want the ruler knuckle sandwich from the Kray nun's, but we went and very soon found ourselves in Madonna's backstage dressing room. Just me, Wanda, 3 dancers and her. I was a bit disappointed though, I thought it would be much posher. It was a shit hole but she was very polite in the shit hole and we exchanged nothing more than "Did you like the show?" "Madonna you are such a great dancer" etc. etc. before it was obvious her politeness had an expiry date and it was about to arrive.

It is only now looking back that the significance of meeting the holy trinity of pop stars comes to me. At that time, I didn't take it in at all, I just went along, hung out, said a few words and left to muck around some more with my friends. But that is some holy trinity to drop into a dinner party now. I was one incredibly lucky teenage girl.

Wanda drove me home from Madonna as quickly as she could, and the next day I got whacked on the knuckles as my homework had of course not been done.

Which wasn't my fault really, the bouncers at Wembley didn't know how to do maths.

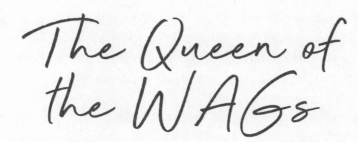

The Queen of the WAGs

"Lizzie is simply the best company and the best laugh you could have with a friend, in any situation."

Bruno Tonioli – Choreographer and Strictly Come Dancing judge

"My beautiful friend Lizzie.

The first time I met her we had a connection, both of us having gone through messy divorces. We became instant friends.

Lizzie has a heart so big it fills me with joy, she is a wonderful mother and a wonderful woman. And a loyal friend.

I truly value my friendship with her, she is simply irreplaceable."

Jo Wood – Great friend and ex-wife of Rolling Stone, Ronnie Wood

In the summer of 2006 a new word was created. It brought with it a tidal wave of reporting that would sell millions of newspapers and magazines around the world.

That word was WAGs or wives and girlfriends to be precise. And wives and girlfriends of footballers to be even more precise. The world went WAG potty.

This wasn't Beatlemania, it was WAGmania and I was in the middle of it to witness the mayhem which first started at the 2006 Germany World Cup finals.

I was, I suppose, in the purest definition *pre WAG* or *diet WAG* as my then husband had retired from football in 2000. The WAG phenomena hadn't started at that point, but I was still part of that 'world' due to my celebrity and sporting connections.

Possibly encouraged by his then girlfriend (the very much self proclaimed 'glamorous' Nancy Dell'Olio an Italian lawyer), Sven-Göran Eriksson the England manager before the start of the 2006 World Cup, proclaimed that he wanted wives and girlfriends to join the Football team's base in Germany to stay with the players during the tournament. The cult of the WAGs arrived onto media centre stage from that moment onwards, a cult entirely made up by the press and fuelled by the press.

The WAG wave continued for another 8 years or so.

I suppose the strong interest already building before the 2006 World Cup shifted into a frenzy when a famous picture of 5 of the WAGs out shopping, walking in a line, through the streets of Baden Baden just after the team had arrived in Germany, got sent around the world's media. The WAGs reluctant leader was none other than Victoria Beckham but she had no real say in the leadership election as she was the wife of one of the world's most famous players and a former 'Spice Girl' to throw in on top. So, the boss role was a certainty whether she wanted it or not. And it was often so difficult to tell with Victoria because she was and still is, so aloof.

But that picture was certainly what really fired it all up.

As news of Baden Baden spread, I spent the next few weeks covering the whole thing for ITV reporting on every movement, every piece of gossip, every bit of fashion the WAGs had on. Ironically, I actually couldn't understand what the frenzy was all about, as despite what you may think and I wouldn't blame you, I am not into all that handbags and shoes thing. But I'm not complaining, it would underpin my career right up until the late summer of 2013.

Everyone seemed to want to read about them. It was a genius creation by the media. The pictures and stories sold millions of copies for them and I rode the tail of that beast. I was on TV everywhere, every show it seemed at one point was reporting it and I even went onto Sky news - it had reached that far in acceptable news worthiness.

The press clambered over toilets, over barriers, over chairs, over each other to get at them. The WAGs were there to support their husbands but got far more attention than them. Many of the girls didn't like it but some definitely played up to the possibilities it would give their profiles and milked the WAG cow's udders for all it was worth. Quite a few went on afterwards to create names for themselves off the back of it.

And who were the original WAG founder members?

Enter stage left wearing strappy summer sandals:

Victoria Beckham, wife of David
Colleen Rooney, wife of Wayne
Cheryl Cole, wife of Ashley
Abby Clancy, girlfriend of Peter Crouch
Alex Curran, wife of Stephen Gerrard
Toni Terry, wife of John
Ellen Rivas, partner of Frank Lampard
Louise Owen, wife of Michael
Carly Zucker, wife of Joe Cole

After the tournament, I had phone call after phone call from various parts of the press on the subject, everyone after my views. It was still hot news as this was the time that footballers, and Chelsea ones in particular, were reported as having affairs. The media came to me because I would get calls from the WAGs themselves about certain incidents, sometimes the WAG men too would call me and therefore I had the inside track. I became the unofficial spokesperson for one or both of them, often going on TV to put their point across to the public.

I was in effect the 'WAGony' aunt which placed me slap bang into the middle of WAG culture and folklore. I had the unique combination of being both a forerunner to them through Jason and also being a TV presenter. That gave me an advantage over anyone else. I was the WAG piggy in the middle and I enjoyed being the piglet for many years.

When the next World Cup came around in 2010 I was a shoe in to be asked to go and report on events for ITV on the ground.

It was to be held in South Africa for the very first time and the WAG phenomena was still going strong with many new members joining the gang whether they really wanted to join or not. That was the problem for any partner of a footballer at that time. If you went out looking lovely you were then a WAG it was as simple as that and you would receive your membership pack from WAG head office a few days later. The *problem* though in 2010 for TV and the press in general was that the new England football manager, Fabio Capello, did not like the thought of WAGs ruining his preparations for matches, and so banned them from being anywhere near his team.

'How selfish putting football first at a football World cup' screamed the world's media, **'Capello's priorities are all wrong.'**

I interviewed Fabio before the team left for the tournament as bizarrely, my friend had got him the flat he rented in London and so a favour was owed and duly called in by Cunders. He openly said to me at the meeting that he was a strong disciplinarian, and he didn't want the hype around the squad that had been seen in

2006. The media and my own selfish interests to one side, you could understand his point of view.

Despite that, I was duly sent by ITV to cover the South African World Cup for them. All was not lost though for the hunting media pack as a number of WAGs were going to go anyway, off their own back, to support their partners. Some though were definitely going, well, to be WAGs. The only difference compared to Germany was that they would not stay at the England hotel itself.

It was so busy, I ended up in that month also doing work for Sky, Channel 5 and overseas broadcasters. The fact they were not with the team made little difference to the reporting frenzy in those 4 weeks and it was full on for all of us reporting, pretty much as soon as we landed.

The biggest issue for me and my team though was accommodation. The crew and I wanted a bit of luxury, (we tried demanding it but we just got laughed at by ITV), and as I had loads of contacts generally out there, Cunders was duly dispatched to blag her way into Sun City. I managed to pull it off but in return I had to promise their hotel manager I would get them coverage by getting the WAGs to show their presence as often as they could.

It wasn't one of the greatest ideas I have ever had. The manager of Sun City at that time, Sue, (aka the blonde Mussolini) was the fiercest and most scary person I had ever met in my entire life and remember I had previously been bashed on the knuckles by the Kray nuns weekly for many years at school. So scared was I of Sue that on the very first day I was begging Emile Hesksy's wife (one of the England players) to come down to the pool to hang out so she could be 'papped' there. But the WAGs very quickly become too scared themselves to talk or do anything, the atmosphere the blonde Mussolini had created was that intense.

She used to bang on my door at all hours, night and day.

"Where are the WAGs darling where are the WAGs?!! I want WAGs!"

I was under the most intense daily pressure to deliver footage for her, because, as I was reminded hourly, we were staying there for free. I was between a rock and a hard place as I didn't want to pressurise the girls too much as many of them were my friends but the constant shouting had me in tears. One day not far into the stay, enough was simply enough.

I hatched both a cunning and well thought out break away plan. So simple it was undoubtedly borderline genius. I would ring another hotel and move us all into there. Told you it was good. And simple. But everywhere was booked of course, it being the World Cup and so blagger Lizzie opened her contacts book up again and luckily happened to know another hotel manager in South Africa, who coincidently ran the best hotel in Johannesburg.

The Saxon.

"Please, please (me oh yeah) George can you help a damsel in distress?" I laid it on in the begging phone call to the Manager.

"Lizzie, of course you can come, it would be such an honour to have you" was his reply, which was frankly massively overdoing my welcome but gratefully accepted nonetheless.

I responded to his generosity as only I could really:

"You are so kind darling, bless you - hang on, silly me, I forgot to mention - I will be bringing 4 friends along with me and they need rooms too I hope you don't mind. Bye!" quickly hanging up!

It really was as simple as asking and we were in. I have no idea how I do it sometimes, this was the busiest ever month for tourists in South African history after all. But I had done a favour for him once

(I'm not telling you what, even though we are already now so close readers) and so a favour return was called in.

His repayment to me though went above and beyond the normal call of Lizzie duty. When I rocked up at The Saxon, I was duly taken up to the penthouse suite which was to be mine for the duration of my World Cup stay apparently, and so therefore now *The Cundy Suite*. I arrived at the penthouse door at the same time as an old familiar face came out of the room (penthouse) next to mine. He was someone who I had been introduced to some time before by Stuart Higgins (from The Sun as I mentioned before).

It was Paddy Harverson, the Royal family's press secretary.

It is fair to say, and to put it mildly, he nearly fainted. Or vomited, it was that close a call. He looked at me, his red sunburnt face turning white very, very quickly, and put his head into his hands making this groaning sound from the depths of his belly, only usually made by the gorilla's of the northern regions of the Congo.

"My good God, no not you, please no, not you" he said flattering me endlessly, "how did you get in here, there are only two rooms on this floor, how, how, why, why?? Noooooooooo not you."

Clearly pleased to see me again, I smiled my best Cundy smile explaining that I knew the boss, told him not to worry, flounced into my suite like Cleopatra of the Nile and slammed the door to *The Cundy Suite* firmly behind me.

Paddy was still outside 2 minutes later with his head in his hands and knees on the floor in some sort of nervous convulsion, as I popped out to get some ice for the bottle of champagne that had been put there for me by the favour-returning Saxon Manager, George.

Everyone should have a George in their life darlings.

Paddy continued the begging to Cleopatra Cundy from *The Cundy Suite* "Please, please (me oh yeah) don't cause any problems, please Lizzie we are trying to keep a low profile and out of any trouble. We don't need to be firefighting any gossip."

And it suddenly dawned on me. All this could only really mean one thing. In the room next to me must be Royalty and Royalty of the proper kind.

Sometime later I came out of *The Cundy Suite's* huge shower and went straight out onto the balcony to gaze at the city. Suddenly I realised I wasn't alone. As I looked to my left there was Prince Harry, Royalty of the proper kind, doing exactly the same thing as me on his balcony. Without the guzzling of champagne down the gob bit.

"Harry!!! how's it going?" were my first ever words spoken to Royalty of the proper kind.

"Good thanks" my new Royal best friend replied, "you out here with all the WAGs?"

A couple of minutes general chat followed and then we both scarpered when we heard Paddy coming into Harry's room. As I came down to go out for an early evening dinner that night with the film crew, I heard a noise coming from the courtyard of the Saxon and I thought to myself "Aye aye Cunders, I smell a party. I will just have a little look and see what's going on" which I did and it was indeed a party.

I blagged my way in, 'quelle surprise' goes up the shout, and just as I'm sipping my first glass of champagne (technically my 8th, but 1st there) 3 lovely smelling, well dressed gentleman came right up beside me. This was not your ordinary threesome, it was a threesome that only ladies with extreme levels of naughty imagination at 2am in the morning could ever dream of.

Prince William, Prince Harry and David Beckham.

Well to be honest darlings I've had worse nights.

"What are you doing here?" said the future King of England to the Queen of the WAGs.

"I've come to cover the World Cup Darling" I replied, thinking about curtsying but realising I may just fall onto the floor at his feet if I attempted it. Which frankly would not be the most dignified thing you could do when meeting the future of the British monarchy.

"Wow Lizzie, you met the King", my friends would screech in high pitched, excited voices, "what happened?"

"Well I fell all over him with my attempt at a dignified bow and curtsey, but apart from that it was fine, thanks so much for asking darling."

For the next hour as I sipped my drink with the 3 most sought after men in the world, indeed dare I say Universe, everyone at the party looked over at me and thought the same thing. How the bloody hell did she blag her way into here and how the bloody hell did that lucky madam then find herself with the 3 Musketeers?

The whole time Paddy is in the distance having kittens. Multiple kittens. Enough to fill a cattery. His whole South African PR plan was looking down the barrel of a Cundy led Armageddon as I hung out with the boys and had a great time.

It is fair to say it was the nuttiest hour in the history of nuts.

Even I realised I couldn't stay uninvited forever and knew I had to go and find my friends who were waiting, now very impatiently, for me to meet them in reception as we had planned to do ages ago.

However, as I was about to step out of the courtyard and into the main hotel, the word goes around to those in the know e.g. the 3 Musketeers and me, that Nelson Mandela was about to arrive.

Right on queue security increased noticeably and there he was, one of the greatest men who had ever lived in the history of earth.

"It's now or never Cunders" came another variation of the rallying call into my mind, and all the training I had in blagging my way into nightclubs, into parties, into everything really came down to this one moment! In fairness it wasn't a tricky blag at all, I just walked very confidently straight up to him and ignored all the security who must have assumed that I was the head of the greeting party itself. Voila as easy as that!

"Hello President Mandela, my name is Lizzie Cundy and I'm reporting on the World Cup for ITV in the UK. I just wanted to say hello to you sir."

And those wondrous, friendly, knowing eyes stared at me for just a split second before he laughed his famous laugh and said:

"It is just so lovely to meet you Lizzie, but tell me please, where are the WAGs, where are they!?"

I giggled. "You tell me sir, I'm trying to find them too!" I replied.

He let out another massive laugh, "Well I wish you good luck!" and that was that he carried on walking as the real greeting party came over to him presumably to not talk about the WAGs.

With my head in a daze from what had happened in the last hour, I found the film crew in the lobby but not the happiest I'd ever seen them, it had to be said. When I was asked why I was so late even for my standards, I simply replied in a tone that befitted my new found place in society, e.g. being a very close friend now of Kings and Presidents and staying in the very exclusive *Cundy Suite:*

"Well, as you asked" I proclaimed in a very regal proclaiming way to my subjects "I was discussing very important matters with Princes William and Harry assisted by David Beckham, and then joined by Nelson Mandela for the conclusion of the summit."

My friend Eric, just looked at me for 5 seconds, shook his head and said:

"Knob."

Which wasn't the appropriate language to use I thought when replying to a person of my obvious new found position in UK, indeed world, but I let him off as I was hungry for a double cheeseburger and he was paying.

Whilst I was at the World Cup, I wanted to do some charity work which has always been important to me so I went into the very heart of Soweto. I brought some South African WAGs with me which would bring a lot of press and therefore highlight some of the issues within Soweto. I have done many visits in my time, but this was simply shocking. Uplifting in many ways but shocking nonetheless. There were many orphanages there but we headed to one in particular. Inside were just the cutest kids you could ever wish to meet, but some were obviously so undernourished that you just wanted to cuddle them, protect them, tell them it would be alright. As a mum, I just couldn't get my head around it all and still to this day I can't.

Everyone wanted a piece of the WAGs in that World Cup. The South African's developed their own WAG gang but it didn't quite work compared to the English version. I opened up shopping malls with some of them, I did everything. It was rent a Cundy for the whole month and came to a head when I was invited onto one of the biggest TV shows in South Africa called Top Billing. Onto the studio floor I go, the crowd start clapping, a few cheers were thrown in but then I looked up and saw they had billed me as Lizzie Cunty. What the hell do you do in that circumstance? Being a silly Cunty, I just soldiered on and didn't try to correct it unlike Cannes a few years later when I did, as you will read later on my darlings.

Which I know is naughty of me to tease you like that, but book foreplay is an acceptable part of English literature don't you know and the Cannes story, a great one! Cunty though is apparently a real surname in South Africa and so no one seemed that bothered I had been called that. So, for a few hours I was a Cunty and remained that way until later that night when I closed the door firmly shut on *The Cunty Suite.*

The pressure in South Africa continued to be immense, to get new stories again and again and I was actually glad when the team got knocked out in the second stage so I could get back to the UK. I'm not sure how I physically did it all looking back to that time but I was living off the excitement and the adrenaline that gives you and of course appreciating all the while just how fortunate I was to have a job that took me to places like that. But some days I felt that the whole WAG world was on my shoulders and this was the time remember I was having real difficulties at home with Jason.

Following my South African adventure, I started to see for the first time WAG charts appearing in the press. I was named as number 10 in the top 10 most annoying WAGs in the UK chart but 18th in the top 50 most beautiful WAGs in Europe poll, so on balance I think that is more than acceptable darlings.

The WAG adventure continued for me even though the World Cup was over.

I first met this guy named Showbiz Simon in 2009 and he was to become a major part of my life from that moment onwards. His real name was Simon Withington or so he said, as no one has ever seen the proof of it. I was doing a TV Show with Jason and he came down to the house to film it, and after he had watched me drink a bottle of champagne he quite rightly pointed out that "I owed him a drink." So off to the pub we both went. He made a point of telling me there that I seemed to be a natural on camera and that I should meet with this guy called Eric Way who was a big TV producer, which I duly did and within a few minutes I was booked up to do a TV show on the WAGs. Or WAGs World to be historically precise.

That led to us making 24 episodes on Sky TV over 4 series filmed from 2009 onwards.

The concept was very simple. I would go and meet with some of them at their houses, generally nose around in all their stuff and then interview them on various things. As I knew most of the girls, and I was a high profile WAG presenter, the belief was I could get the best out of them, which I suppose was a fair assumption to make at that time.

First up was Alex Best who had married the coolest and first superstar footballer, George Best. My tactic was to bring a bottle of champagne for the ladies which always works to loosen up anyone and the first show was one of the best as they had only just split and everything was still very raw, especially for Alex. There were a few tears when I interviewed her which unashamedly made for good TV.

I had known George myself fairly well for some time. He gate-crashed my 21st birthday which is one hell of an opening line to tell anyone as an ice breaker at a dinner party. I had first seen him in a gym I was using at Dover Street, which I had blagged my way into naturally, as I had been on a shoot there for a tanning cream product one day, and just sort of then claimed the gym as mine for months afterwards. Angie Best, George's first wife, walked in one day with a very young Callum Best, who is a good friend now, but he was a total 'Best brat' that day. A very cute 'Best brat' though it had to be said.

He was running around saying things like "Don't look at me, don't come near me" which I can tell you now he wouldn't say to any lady today!

I got so friendly with the owners that I proclaimed, as the supreme diva blagger that I am, I would have my 21st birthday there in their private members bar section. They didn't refuse and so I did. That night George turned up out of the blue and quite rightly pointed out he didn't need an invite as he was, well, George Best. Fair enough. I have a recollection now that he was trying to chat up my grandmother that night which may be wrong, but more likely it is right as George was George, and my nan was blonde. (G+B=yes) is an equation they should have taught in a school classroom back then.

I had Angie Best on that first series too and she was just so sad about George passing away as she wished she could have saved him. A lot of us did as well, but no one ever could have done. It was quite an emotional chat and Angie, remember was the original Queen of the WAGs, way before anyone knew that word or world ever existed. She had bragging rights over everyone therefore, though she didn't really care that she did.

The only WAG interview which don't go quite so well, or at least sometime after, was with Alicia Douvall who had been a partner of the Manchester United footballer Dwight Yorke. Which many ladies had been, it is fair to say, the naughty red devil! The TV show went ok apart from yours truly having to walk over rabbit poo everywhere in her house when I arrived, which was simply disgusting.

Sometime after the filming, her and I were on an ITV debate about husbands of WAGs and I defended Ashley Cole over the latest rumour to surface about him. She didn't see eye to eye with me. At all. When the filming was over, we went back to the green room and she went for me, saying what I had argued on Ashley's behalf was insulting to her and that I had 'made her look bad' for the simple reason apparently, I hadn't agreed with her.

She then decided that words were not getting her point over enough, and so threw a cup of hot tea over my white jeans (white jeans being very much acceptable on a lady). I'm still not sure to this day if she was being 'playful' or not, but the press had a field day about it nonetheless. Ashley at least thanked me the next day for giving his side of the story but it just once again showed that the WAGs were very much a talking point in society at that time.

Of course, nowadays the WAGs are looked down upon scornfully by the media, but the media created them and the media made money from them. Every paper in this country would have featured them at some point and sold many copies because of them, some millions more no doubt. The hypocrisy was, and still is, therefore everywhere. It was a phenomenon, there is no doubt about it and therefore deserves to have been documented at that time as a reflection on society, for good or for bad.

As the years went on, I continued to try and protect both the ladies and their partners including one night when a very famous WAG keyed her husband's car outside a bar. I was there and genuinely tried to stop her but she was determined, rational thought had left the building and she was going to do it no matter what.

I had been given the name Queen of the WAGs by the press after I had organised a WAG charity fashion show not long after the 2006 World Cup. The mayhem there that night showed to me what a presence in this country they now had, and would continue to have. The 2006 World Cup was therefore not a one hit WAG wonder, as Wimbledon High Street was pretty much shut down that night and before the show had even finished, it was on the front page of the Evening Standard quickly followed with coverage all over the other national newspapers the following day.

It was there that Richard Desmond, boss of OK! magazine, really started to come into my life for the first time. He said to me at that show that I was "Going to be handy" in the future for him as "no one wanted Brad and Angelina" on the cover anymore of OK! they wanted the WAGs. I have known and worked with him ever since and still to this day remains my terrifying friend.

In the early summer of 2013, I got a call totally out of the blue about joining a West End show which was about to start in a month's time. A regular every day call, therefore. The show was about the WAGs and had been touring the fringe theatres around the country. I was asked to come and audition right away which I said yes to, as I was hugely impressed it was being produced by Paul Nicholas, the star of the TV show Just Good Friends. He had also been in the original production of Cats in Drury Lane.

I turned up at the theatre and must be the only person in history applying for the main part in a West End musical to utter the immortal words to a laughing producer:

"I can't sing darling, is that going to be a problem?"

I kept saying to all of them "I'm not sure I can do this" but I read a little bit of the script at the back of the theatre, and that seemed to warm them up to the idea of me being cast as the lead role. It needed to warm them up let me tell you, as the back of any theatre is freezing cold, dingy, dark and very small. Not the glamorous place you may think it is!

I left the audition, was in a taxi going to another appointment when I got a call from the production team saying "Come back Lizzie, we want you, rehearsals start next week, and by the way, the Evening Standard are here would you mind awfully chatting to them as they plan to do an immediate scoop on it."

Blimey!

"I will call you back in one minute" I just about managed to get my startled voice to say:

"Shall I, shan't I, shall I, shan't I" I chanted to myself in a Hare Krishna type of way, as the taxi driver just looked at me in his rear view mirror as if I was a nutcase, which of course I was and still very much am.

I rang them back.

"I'm in, I will be back in 10 minutes, and God help you."

I happened to see Andrew Lloyd Webber that night who said I had made the right decision. His advice to me then in view of my lack of singing ability was to just "Camp it up." Perfect for me, as I did that every day in my normal life anyway.

I turned up on the first day of rehearsals and felt immediately intimidated. The cast all knew that I was an outsider and they were battle hardened stage performers. I was totally out of my comfort zone and it showed. First up we all gathered in a circle and the main song to start the show off was to be the opening part of the very first rehearsal too. It didn't help my nerves or indeed my comfort zone, which had buggered off down Shaftesbury Avenue and wasn't coming back.

So, there I was about to *sing* that song with everyone staring at me. They all seemed to be thinking "What is she doing here, what has she done to deserve this?" and none more so than the man due to play my lover in the show, Tim Flavin, who had won an Olivier Award in 1984. A great achievement, but 30 years on, he was still playing off it. I felt many times during the whole show's run that I should say to him, "Let it go, just lighten up" but it wouldn't have done any good because from that first practice, it was as if he didn't want the show to do well at all.

"Oh, you have a lovely sweet singing voice" they lied to me on mass at the end of the first rehearsal, but we all knew that I needed help. I got singing lessons immediately from Tee Green, the voice coach to the stars, and topped that up with help on the dancing from Arlene Phillips and guidance generally from Stacey Haynes.

And what did I learn? Well, wine and champagne dries your throat apparently, so there you go, that is a fact which may come in useful in the future for you darlings.

The whole lead up to opening night and the resentment shown to me wasn't helped with both the show photoshoots and the general press interest being centred around me, which was obviously going to happen in view of my WAG history and TV exposure. What they seemed to forget was I was getting publicity not for me, but for the show. Big publicity. In the end I tried to win them round by just working hard. Theatre word is bitchy but I was there everyday putting the effort in to show them I was a grafter and not just there for the ride. At the same time, I continued to lead the PR, arranging a launch party, getting us on morning TV, and getting massive amounts of extra press. Eventually it worked. The bond of work, well, bonded us all together.

All except the non-existent bond with the man cast to be my man in the show. There was no Mr Lover Lover going on there, in fact no, nothing going on there! The contempt he had for me was highlighted for everyone to see in all its glory on the second night of the shows' 6 week run.

As I came out on stage that night with my *prince*, I fell badly, and the gallant knight in shining armour that he was just stepped right over me and walked on, in what I assume was an attempt to hog the limelight for himself at that very moment. Well, he had won an Olivier Award 30 years before, so fair enough readers that gave him the right to do it. I had forgotten to rub my soles with chalk to stop my shoes slipping, which is an old theatre trick and I paid the heavy price for it.

I eventually rose, giving my best sleeping beauty awakening performance, the crowd cheered and I carried on which was bloody hard as the pain in my arse, no readers, not the man who had won an Olivier Award 30 years before pain in the arse, but the actual pain in my arse, was excruciating as that is where I had landed when I had fallen to the floor. The show must go on so I carried on as best I could, as if nothing had happened, which is hard when you are walking around with severe bottom issues let me tell you darlings. And the man who had won Olivier Award 30 years before? He didn't say a single word to me about it afterwards. Not one word. A bit like a man after sex then ladies!

The reviews for the show were on the whole not good. They were never going to be though in the traditional fortress of West End Theatre.

I just laughed out loud when I read these:

'This is all such well-trodden territory that it requires sharpness of wit, lightness of touch and an impudent, swaggering style to have a chance of engaging. It has none of these things.'

'An extra fiver per ticket gets you a large glass of house wine and you'll probably need it if you're going to enjoy this musical.'

'It's not often that you hear the word affection rhymed with erection but that's the kind of show this is.'

But the press were wrong. The public loved it. I only had 3 weeks rehearsals but night after night I pulled off the highest note in the opening song and I believe we all did a great job. Every matinee and evening performance was sold out, with hen parties and the gay community especially supporting us during our run. The show lasted for 6 weeks between July and August, the length of time it was supposed to, which I'm sure delighted the critics who had tried to torpedo it at the very start.

I was knackered though when the curtain fell on the very last performance. As everyone was. I didn't get paid much for the work but what an experience it had been, what an adventure. I had 3 offers to do other West End shows following WAGs the Musical but theatre just wasn't going to be for me in the long-term. With two shows a day it would have been impossible to have carried on my normal life and do that too.

That period of my life was now over.

The country was all wagged out, and none more so than me.

Two Tribes

"Oh, my darling friend and shining light.

Lizzy Cundy is a very special friend to me. It's one of those friendships where we share the same energetic vibration, or let's say, empathic blending occurs. When we meet, the laughter, sarcasm and wit begins until the point we can literally cry with laughter because our sense of humour is the same.

She is one of the funniest, genuine and loving friends anyone can have. She doesn't miss a beat. Along the same lines, she is always upbeat even during times of turmoil in her private life. She will still see the glass half full and find humour in a negative situation.

Just give her a glass of wine and a dress that reveals almost all and she's in top form. She's a very happy girl with a certain sex appeal which draws a lot of people in.

How can anyone not like Lizzy?"

Joy Desmond – great friend and wife of Richard Desmond, boss of OK! magazine

Break life down and there are I suppose, simplistically, two things that define the type of human you are.

Are you good or are you bad?

Or in some cases are you good or are you evil?

There are two tribes of human behaviour in this world and I have experienced the very best and very worst of each.

It was at drama school that I first met Wanda Walker. She was 12 and had been diagnosed with Cystic Fibrosis from birth, which is a disorder that mostly affects the lung.

Within a few days of becoming her friend I was 'warned' not to be as she had been told that she would only live to the age of 14, and so therefore "Best not be friends eh" for my sake. For my sake? What about her sake? It was exactly the reason I should be her friend.

She was so funny but had a terrible cough most of the time, which in part then caused her to have a really dirty laugh, which then just made you laugh even more.

She mainly laughed at herself though. She had been dealt the worst set of cards life could give you, but she used to take the mickey out of that fact again and again. When I went into hospital once with some flowers for Wanda, as we believed it was touch and go if she would make it through the night, she greeted me with the classic "What are they for Lizzie, has someone died?." We grew up together and went through her illness together but no matter what was happening to Wanda she put everyone at ease. Her illness did not stop her living her life.

The illness could not be ignored though. When she was 27, some 14 years after the first prognosis of how long she would live for, it was clear that my best friend was gradually slipping away. Her only chance was to have a heart and lung transplant. In classic Wanda style when she found out the organs would be coming from someone in Spain, she proclaimed that she would wake up as 'Pedro the waiter' and did she really have to go through with it? But she did, Wanda had gotten so desperately thin, she had to.

The massively complicated transplant operation didn't go to plan and complications developed quickly. The word got out that she would need a lot of blood and quickly. Within a few minutes of that news breaking, hundreds of people in Richmond came out in support of her and donated blood. It was the most incredible and moving sight I had ever seen.

But we lost her that night.

I will never forget, with tears flowing down my cheeks, sprinting down the corridor of Harefield Hospital with my great friend Helen Chaikin in a desperate attempt to see my sweet Wanda alive. For just one last time. To hold her hand, stroke her hair and tell her how much I loved her. For just one last time.

But I didn't make it. There would be no more last times.

She had just passed away.

My Wanda had gone and for hours I simply couldn't breathe. I'm not sure I even wanted to breathe. I would never laugh with my best friend ever again.

Wanda lived life to the full, and I lived it with her. We had a friendship so deep that we often didn't need to say anything, we could just sit together in silence and enjoy being with each other and our dreams. It was a once in a lifetime special bond from a once in a lifetime special friend. She was always so incredibly brave, so dignified and so full of positivity.

She lived each day as if it was her last, knowing eventfully it actually would be.

I miss her even now and I think about that amazing inspiring lady every single day.

For a month after her death I could hardly get out of bed I was that heartbroken. But two things happened after she died that showed to me, in spirit at least, she was still part of my life.

On the night of her death, when I eventually got home, the wind had blown some white feathers into my house through the windows I had left open.

White feathers were Wanda's symbol, she loved them.

And then some time after her death, I was on a plane flying to interview Vinnie Jones in LA and the man who sat down next to me on that flight was unbelievably Dr Yacoub, who had performed the surgery on Wanda the day she had passed away. He told me that even he had donated his blood that day to try and bring her round. As emotional as it was for me talking about her with him on that flight, I knew she had placed him next to me.

What an amazing man he was. He had tried everything to save her the day she died, that I am 1,000% sure of.

What I am also 1,000% sure of is that when I got off the plan in LA, Wanda was with me once more.

Another of my friends died soon after Wanda. Nikki Ferguson had encouraged me to go to drama school with her when I was 9, and looking back I know those years in acting classes contributed enormously to the confidence I now have in my life. I was also at *normal* school with her. She was a great friend but would often have a touch of sadness about her even when she was at that age.

We used to practice all the 80's dance moves in her bedroom and generally muck around day after day, night after night. Those are the happiest times of your life when you look back. Many years later we were still very close but often it felt like she was remote, not just from me, but from life. Somewhere else in her thoughts.

I had just given birth to Josh when I heard the news that Nicki had been found hanging from an apple tree in her garden after committing suicide.

I simply hadn't spotted the warning signs. I was to
newborn son and wrapped up in all things mothe
was nothing I could have done anyway I suppose
set on ending their lives they simply will.

A year later I also lost my dad to a heart attack. He was just 69.

These deaths, of people so much part of my world, just toughened
me up more and more. It gave me experience on how to deal with
utter despair and how to pick yourself back up off of the floor to fight
back again once more.

Though I already had some 'training' in that from something which
happened one night in 1984.

Out of the blue, one day that year, a celebrity and very well respected
manager in the industry by the name of Tony Fox called my modelling
agency and said he needed someone with personality as well as
looks for some TV projects he had moving forward. The agency
office said they had just the person, aka me, and they arranged a
time for me to go and present my work to him.

His office was impressive. Well, to a 16 year old it was, as on the
wall hung row after row of pictures of Radio 1 DJs, who in the 1980's
especially, were household names in the UK. The meeting was very
general, lots of chit-chat about nothing really, the weather, the
fashion of the time, but every few minutes I had compliment after
compliment given to me, which at that moment in my life I was not
used to at all. I only had experience of teenage boys saying teenage
things to me and my father did not like to praise me at all, he came
from the other side of parenting where tough love on pretty much
every occasion was deemed to be far more appropriate.

At the end of the half hour meeting, Tony told me that as I was so
impressive, so naturally talented, I should do a film of myself going
about my daily life so he could then use it to show his TV contacts

ust how good I was on camera. He seemed totally sure that I would be a star and I needed to make the jump now from modelling to presenting. To be honest, I hadn't ever really thought about it up to that point, I was still riding the wave I had been on since I had been discovered by Peter Stringfellow at the age of 14.

My excitement at the thought of being on film was soon extinguished though when I tried to carry home the huge video camera I had bought to film the masterpiece, which would of course become 'Lizzie the Movie' and released in cinemas. At this time, in the mid 1980's, technology as you know it now was not technology as we knew it then, and the iPhone equivalent in 1985 was a ten pound video camera the size of Mike Tyson's bottom. It was only with great determination that I managed to carry it all the way home to begin my filming.

My dad was not impressed to say the least. He never was by anything that I did really, and certainly not by the meeting I had just had, the opportunity, the camera, the carrying it home, nothing.

"I'm not helping you film that, if you want to be in the industry you need to learn how hard it is yourself" he lectured me on the subject, not for the first time, which frankly just hugely pissed me off once again as Tony Fox had been so sure I was going to be a huge star. He had showered me with compliment after compliment to prove his point.

My father not being impressed just made me want to make a film even more. I wrote out a script, planned the way I would look and just as I was about to drag a friend in to undertake the monumental task of holding the huge camera, my father relented and agreed to help. In the end he was impressed by what I had achieved, as he occasionally was, but as it was always so tough to get him to that point I often just didn't even bother to start to.

When I presented 'Lizzie the Movie' to Tony though he simply loved it. Overly loved it, proclaiming once again that:

"Lizzie, with your gorgeous looks and natural charm you are made for TV presenting. You will be a huge star babe I can personally make sure of that."

I was becoming more and more impressed by anything he said to me. I didn't ask many questions at that second meeting, there was no need to. Tony said I would be a huge star so that was that. Instead of a contract to sign though, he suggested to me at the end that we needed to go out for dinner together to talk about my future properly.

I agreed on the spot. Seemed a great idea to me.

My sister was far from impressed though when I told her later that night.

"Lizzie this just doesn't feel right" was her advice that I instantly ignored. I just didn't see what she saw. She didn't know Tony like I did and he was obviously a great manager by the number of male Radio 1 DJ's he looked after at that time.

The next day I relented in part and said I would have dinner with him at the restaurant my sister ran in Richmond, not that far from where I lived. She was still not happy but that made no difference to me whatsoever.

During the dinner a few days later, Tony Fox promised me the world. The total world. He upped his praise of me to unbelievable levels.

"You will be in great shows, the biggest shows" he said, talking about my great presenting skills again and again. "You are made to be a TV star, it's in you and you can be one right now, this instant. trust me."

And I did. I had started to really believe him. It must be true because he had said it to me again and again. On top of that he had explained that any recommendation of his would be gold dust for me and as he seemed to like me, I must therefore be a shoe in to the world of television.

We finished the meal and it had been a very good night all round, I thought. As we walked outside, he pointed to his big Mercedes and said to me ever so casually:

"I will drop you home sweetheart."

When I explained I was just 10 minutes away and there was no need to go to that trouble, he then became insistent, his hook being the fact he wanted to run through some final things with me about my career before the night was over. I felt a sense of danger for the first time, but my naive legs still walked to his big Mercedes and got in.

As we came closer to my house he suddenly parked the car at the end of the long road I lived in, a good 400 metres away from my front door. I remember thinking oh damn I hadn't explained where I lived properly to him.

"No, I'm further down the street Tony" pointing to the far end of the road.

He had other plans though. He no doubt had them from the moment he first met me.

"I know Lizzie, I know sweetheart. Look I just want to talk to you a bit more, you know, before we say goodnight, go over the key points again" he said, adding for impressive effect a line he had probably used 1,000 times before "In the years ahead you could become the biggest star we have you know."

And there he was, reminding me again of how huge I would be.

Brainwashing me.

Grooming me.

Getting himself off on how powerful he thought he undoubtedly was.

In an instant the whole atmosphere changed. His sleazy face turned towards me, his eyes which had seemed so welcoming and friendly when I had first met him, became darker, sinister, and the smile of a kind manager with my best interests at heart had now turned inwards to be a smile of determination and lust. He licked his lips, looked down my whole body slowly, staring at me all the time and then rested his hand onto my knee.

A scared, vulnerable, barely 16 year old's knee.

I was petrified. It was the worst horror film scene imaginable but this was now real life horror. I knew what this now all meant. Rape. I cannot begin to tell you what that sheer rush of panic felt like as his words came to me:

"Come on Lizzie, let's do it" he whispered in what was the most disgusting and creepy tone of voice I had ever heard.

He stroked my knee with his grubby sweaty hands and carried on with, "You can have this the easy way baby or the hard way. You can fast track your career right now if you are a clever girl, so come on you know what the right decision is to make here, you could be a huge star and I can help you get there. It's a tough business but I can make it so much easier for you... but only, only baby if I like you."

I was breathless. I was worthless. I couldn't speak. I couldn't scream. I couldn't move. My body had gone into a total deep freeze sense of shock. We had by chance parked outside my friend Helen's house and I could hear Kajagoogoo playing from her open window as he then leaned forward and tried to kiss me moving his hand inch by inch further up my leg, trying to slowly force the other one open at the same time.

"Hey girl move a little closer" sang one of my idols Limahl, as 'Too Shy' played in the distance.

'Hush hush, eye to eye' came through the air to me as Fox's face moved ever closer to mine.

'Mmmmm baby try' the music played on as the rapist now came at me with full force in his oh so powerful big Mercedes.

In his mind this wasn't rape it was a business contract. No need for any more small talk for Tony Fox, the justification for what he was about to do to me was already there in his sexually twisted mind. He no doubt believed he was doing me a favour.

There is no foreplay in rape simply because it is rape. And he believed I should let him fast track a career for myself by opening my 16 year old legs to him. His sexual violation of my innocence moved up a notch as he grabbed my hands, either to stop me stopping him or to force them on the parts of his body which would gave him sexual pleasure. He moaned in satisfaction. I was still frozen but somehow struggling a pathetic struggle against a man intent on raping a 16 year old girl.

'Please Helen my dear friend, please, please look out and see me, look out the window and help me' pleaded my mind as Kajagoogoo finished the last verse from her upstairs, safe, bedroom.

No doubt that is what happened back then to many girls by many men who believed they were so powerful. Pre-Weinstein, well, there was Weinstein. There has always been Weinstein. Men in high positions who believe their own fake powerful minds will *ask* for sexual favours in return for promotions. They aren't really asking they will just seek to take what they believe is rightfully theirs to have. Because they are rapists.

When did I agree that my body was yours to have Mr Fox??

He died in 2008. May he rot in hell for all of eternity.

From somewhere in the car that night God gave me some strength and I managed to punch him.

You are not having me you disgusting rapist scumbag!

Then I hit him again but this time in the balls and as he lurched forward and backwards in pain I managed to scramble out of the car just as he made one last attempt to grab me with his sweaty lecherous rapist hands. I ran. I couldn't breathe but still I ran. I didn't stop, didn't look back, just ran.

I was too scared to tell anyone but my friends Wanda and Helen. I didn't want to tell my family as they had warned me and I felt so embarrassed, ashamed and dirty. He was just too powerful a figure in showbiz to tell anyone else, and like many others this may have happened to, I was worried I would never get work after that if I did. He tried to get in touch with me in the weeks after but I never retuned any calls or messages of his.

What happened to me isn't a reflection on mankind, it is an example of how power can corrupt some people. Most men I have met from the 'powerful' to the 'normal' would never dream of doing what he tried to do to me, but every so often it does happen, it can happen and society has now woken up to that fact.

To this day I have never told my family this story. I have absolutely no idea why.

Hollywood

"People only see the party Lizzie. That is not the real Lizzie.

I have seen her fame rise and rise. In 2010 she was occasionally on TV, now she is the go-to person on ITV for a lot of things in the morning.

She has loads of people who latch on to her who are desperate to be famous, and she can't say no, and doesn't want to say no as she wants to be liked. Many of her so-called friends are takers, and because she is so friendly that they instantly think they are her best friend.

Lizzie is the Queen of the blaggers. When Shirley Valentine was on, we went around Anthea Turner's apartment to watch the second episode, but when we turned up Anthea wasn't there and Lizzie at that time didn't have a key. This would usually result in leaving the building and going home to watch it, but Lizzie being Lizzie flounced up to the security and blagged her way into Anthea's apartment without any ID or anything.

The only time I have not seen it work for her was at the Oscars. We didn't have any access to it, we were there for general coverage, but she was determined to get in but didn't, despite her trying to manoeuvre past every police cordon they had set up around Sunset Boulevard.

She could have made it big in the States I'm convinced of that. They went 'ga ga' for her but she won't leave her boys, she is a home bird deep down.

I actually think she may believe now that a man would hold her back in her drive to advance her career.

She is not very good with money and she is always, always late.

Lizzie sacrificed her acting and modelling career to get married, and it's my opinion that had she not taken the family path, she'd have been even more famous than she is now. The fact that she gave it all up to be a wife and mother, just goes to show how unselfish she is."

Simon Withington aka Showbiz Simon - freelance TV producer

Stephen Dorff

It was the Olympic summer of 2012 and my 17 year old niece Mimi was staying with me for a few days.

We were driving in my car along the Kings Road, me trying to be cool and Mimi just rolling her eyes at everything I was saying to be cool, when Cheryl, her of the opening Mickey Rourke story fame, calls and purrs:

"Where are you my darliiiiiiiiiinnnnnnnng?"

Before I could mutter any sort of sensible reply she said:

"I have someone very famous with me who you simply must meet darliiiiiiiiiiinnnnnnng and I insist you come over here right now. I'm not saying who it is except this is Hollywoooooooooood."

Cheryl had moved on from Blakes Hotel and was looking after the 5 star Cadogan situated at the very top of Sloane Square, 5 minutes away from where I was. We parked up and went into the hotel's courtyard garden where Mr Hollywoooooooooooooood and Cheryl the fixer were having a drink. Mr Hollywoooooooooooooooood was very scruffy with black Ray Bans on, tatty jeans and he was just about to eat his salad which had arrived. She introduced me to him as the Queen of the Red carpet as I had been doing lots of TV interview work at the award shows at that time.

He takes his glasses slowly down, not saying a word yet and stares at me.

Mr Hollywoooooooooooood was in fact Stephen Dorff, of the 'Power of One' and 'Blade' fame. He immediately seemed so endearing and sweet towards me.

"I can't eat in front of you I will leave it until later baby."

Left: My special chum, Anne Summers boss Jackie Gold celebrating her beating cancer. My inspiration!

Below: Hosting the film festival.

Right: My bestie Bruno Tonioli at Simon Cowell's dog charity event 'K9 Friends Barbados'.

Below: LA fun at Roland Emmerich's New Years Eve party with Paul, Bruno and my son Josh.

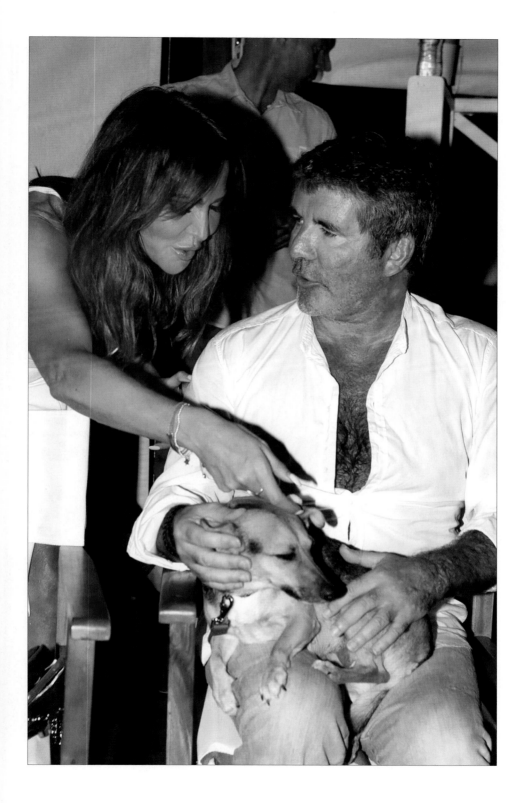

Above: Simon Cowell with 'Daisy' his newly adopted.
She only had eyes just for Simon.

Right: Old chum Jeremy Kyle. We both supported each other through our marriage splits. Great guy!

Below: Charlotte Mears, me, Danielle Lloyd and Alex Best The WAG Fashion show that went mental.

Cheryl, Coleen and Posh cheer England on, 2006

Above: Press... WAG mania.

Above: My great friend Joy Desmond, Richard Desmond and their daughter Angel.

Left: Hosting the auction at Simon Cowell's dog charity bash, Barbados 2018.

Below: One of our many funny nights out at the Chelsea Ivy with my good pals Bruno, Paul and Sara Dallin from Bananarama.

Right: Naughty lunch with good pals Anthea Turner and Bruno.

Below: On the buses for the Pink Ribbon charity event. Could not believe my mates awful pink boots!

Left: Royal Ascot 2018.

Right: Having fun with my friends Tonia Buxton and Titanic star Billy Zane

Left: On my way to the National Television Awards via the tube. Had a car accident on the way to the awards and had to jump on the tube in this gown... got a few looks!!

Right: My good friend
Jason Gardiner at
Julien Macdonald's
fashion show.

Below: My oldest
dearest pals
Jason Gardiner,
Cheryl Howard,
Lisa Voice, my fellow
co-star from
Shirley Valentine at my
fave club - Arts Club.

Left: At West Ham v Chelsea with fabulous friend Jackie Gold.

Below: The loves of my life, my boys and niece Mimi.

Right: With pal Rylan Clark on 'Big Brother's Bit on the Side'.

Below: Reading the news sitting on Rylan's knee!

Left: My buddies
Boris and Lily Becker
at their birthday bash
in Wimbledon.

Right: Sam Fox
and me winning
Celebrity Soccer Six.

Left: Love doing the
Sky debates with
Kay Burley. She's one
of the most supportive
lovely ladies I know.

Above and Below: Having a laugh on the Shirley Valentine show.

Left: Taking a selfie with the Shirley Valentine crew.

Below: Our greek restaurant owner Yanni.

Right: Bruno and I with our friend Lorna. Bruno likes to wear even less clothes than me.

Below: Celebrating my return with Bruno and Paul.

Left: A barbeque at Bruno's.

Right: Josh and Bruno having a laugh at Bruno's barbeque.

Left: The fun show that gets all the showbiz headlines, here with my co-host Stephen Leng.

Right: My best friend Wanda I lost at 27 years old.

Below: Yoga on the set of Shirley Valentine with Aggie.

Left: Vickie White my manager and great friend. Celebrating me landing the part on the Shirley Valentine show.

Below: On the set of Strictly with Craig Revel Horwood, Keren Woodward and Sara from Bananarama.

Right: At the panto with Arlene Phillips who helped me massively with my musical training. Comedian Tim Vine photobombing in the background.

Below: One of the greatest occasions. My dearest friend Eamonn Holmes recieves his OBE. With wife Ruth and daughter Rebecca. Great friends to me.

Left: Out for dinner with Al Pacino on the night it all went south.

Below: My first meeting with Al.

Right: Having great fun with designer Julien Macdonald.

Below: Having a giggle on the set of This Morning with Eamonn and Ruth.

Left: With my good friends Denise Welch and Sheryl Howard at David Gest's funeral. It was a great celebration of his life!

Below: Body confident. Showing what I've got!

My tips for giving yourself a boost

● Find clothes that flatter you. You always feel better on a night out when you love your outfit. Don't follow the trends if they don't suit you.

● Be original, because there's only one you.

● Exercise. Not just for your outer-self, but for your inner-self, too. If you've got time to chat on the phone, then you've got time to do a bit of exercise. It makes you feel amazing.

● Surround yourself with trusted friends and people you love. Hanging out with my boys always makes me feel happy.

Lizzie with her two sons, Jack and James

She explains, "I'd liked this boy for ages and he liked me. But one day he said, 'Lizzie, your legs look like sticks in a bucket.' You so lovely, but you look so ill.' I went home and looked in the mirror for the first time, really saw myself. My face haunted, my eyes wide and my cheeks sucked in. I looked ran downstairs and mum I needed a m

HAPPY ENDIN
She adds, "I don't his comment res me so much, but realise what I'd by my body. I was k I went to a doctor and he put me o

She's known for her risqué outfits

Right: With David at the ITV studios a few weeks before he died.

Below: With my friend the lovely Christine Lampard. Having my famous make-under on the Lorraine Kelly show.

These were his first words to me, the romantic effect of which was lost after 3 seconds when he in fact tucked into the lettuce like it was a Big Mac. As he scoffed away, he kept moving his sunglasses up and down trying to be cool but coming across more like Eric Morecambe every time he did it. Which just made him even more cute in my eyes. Mimi was in *hyperventilating mode* as unbeknown to me, Stephen was in the Britney Spears video for 'Everytime' the 2004 mega hit of hers. He had been chosen for that promo from thousands of people apparently, but I only knew her hit 'Baby One More Time'. That one featured the famous schoolgirl video which had inspired many a lady crush and requests from men for Cosplay Saturday evening once a month.

After half an hour or so of courtyard chit-chat, Cheryl whispered to me, probably pre-planned, "You must see his suite" and added the rather ridiculous comment, "in case you wanted to book it for yourself of course for the future."

Very unlikely my darling.

"Sorry kids, that private education your father is not paying for is on hold for 4 months, but all is not lost as I'm having bubbles with everyone in my penthouse at the Cadogan a week Saturday."

Once we got into the room, I have to say though, that credit where credit is due, it was some suite! The suite of all suite's. A bit like the green triangle in the quality street tin is.

We made small talk for a few minutes and all the time Cheryl, like a mother hen and not like the pimp I thought she now was, was asking him to pack as he had to leave for a flight shortly. There were clothes everywhere. Dirty clothes everywhere. It wasn't the greatest *sell* of a suite I have to say "Here is the TV, surrounded by dirty socks" but I got the flavour of how magnificent it was.

Then, all of a sudden, I was dragged (dare I say sucked) into the suite's bathroom by what I can only describe as a human hoover, finding myself alone with Stephen for the first time.

"I have to kiss you, I just have to kiss you!" he triumphantly declared. Hail Caesar baby.

Romance ignored, because it is sooooo overrated in this Tinder age, he pulled me towards him and started kissing me as if it was the last kiss before the end of the world arrived in 5 minutes time. The bizarre nature of the situation was highlighted even further when all the time we were in there I could hear Cheryl outside saying to Mimi "Look at the simply wooooooooonderful curtains daaaaaaaarling and here are the woooooooooooonderful footstalls" as she pitched the suite of all suite's to a 17 year old student earning £6 an hour at the weekends.

In the bathroom, Stephen was wild. It was wild. I was wildly bowled over. Then suddenly there was a bang. And not a subtle bang either but a BANG BANGABANG. His bottom had hit the electric toothbrush by the sink and it had spun crashing to the floor. BANG. The banging toothbrush didn't stop Stephen trying his best to bang me though and the toothbrush, now turned on because of its fall from grace, just sounded like a vibrator as it went around the bathroom floor in search of a mouth.

I was 'rescued' by the concerned Cheryl who suddenly ruined Stephen's zero bang chance by tapping on the door and sheepishly asking "My daaaaaarling are you ok?" All I managed to mutter in reply was "uuurrgrgrgh" as his tongue was stuck somewhere in the depths of my throat, so much so I thought at one stage I would have to call the fire brigade to release me. But she must have taken "uuurrgrgrgh" as "yes I'm fine thanks for asking my darling and don't worry about the vibrator either, we don't need any new batteries for it" because she continued the sales pitch on the 17 year old and ignored any Dyson shenanigans in the suite of all suite's bathroom.

I finally emerged looking like I had been in a tornado with my hair everywhere and Cheryl simply said "Oh my darling, I think he is quite taken by you." Which I suppose readers he was.

I was quite flattered to be honest. I was on/off with Danny Cipriani and another man's attention at the time I was off with Danny, just boosted my confidence still feeling the aftershock of my break-up with Jason. And this attention was the raw, explosive, kind and that is hard to ever ignore. I had only left The Cadogen for 5 minutes and back driving in my car when my phone rang. Cheryl had obviously forgotten the unforgettable rule of asking for approval before handing out a lady's phone number.

"I'm in London all the time honey, I simply must see you again" Stephen insisted. And I agreed. Hit me baby one more time.

But before then we spent a few months in a long distance text relationship. It was during those exchanges though that he started to show the early signs of possessiveness, sending me messages like *"You are not texting back quickly enough Lizzie, you have forgotten about me"* forgetting himself of course that LA is 8 hours behind the UK, and I wasn't setting my alarm for 3am just so I could send a *"how are your darling?"* text.

But the texts did get rather naughty nonetheless, and those one's I would have set my alarm for 3am to receive anytime. I would say a 6.8 on the naughty scale ladies in case you were interested.

I suppose I was therefore in a semi relationship with him, in between being in a semi-relationship with Danny, but the two never overlapped. I would never have allowed it to. Just like with Danny, Stephen and I never said we were 'together' but there were signs some days that we definitely were. But it was part of the journey for me to get back to being with someone properly, and all the joy and heartbreak that brings.

When he was with me I have no idea if he cheated on me or not. But I suspect I know the answer. I have had 12 sexual relationships in my life, and a friend of mine out of the blue asked me a question the other day which floored me for a minute.

"How many of those men do you think have cheated on you?"

I sat staring into space in total silence before I replied to him. Deep in thought. With a tear growing in my eye, I looked down and whispered:

"All of them."

Which is either a reflection on me or on mankind or both. I seem to go for dangerous men and despite the obvious warnings my friend's give me, I am naïve in relationships. I believe I can change a dangerous man. That makes me vulnerable and vulnerability always ends with a broken heart. You chase love like that, but you know it's a chase for fools. You get knocked over but you put your lip gloss back on and start again, before the wave of self pity hits you smack in the chops once more. But ladies it's not us. It's them. We could be a supermodel with an Einstein brain, cook like Nigella Lawson and be an award winning access all areas of the body porn star, but men will still find a way to think another women is better for them, even for one night.

I have never cheated on any man, putting to one side what you do as a teenager. I have never strayed with any married man whilst I was single. I would not do that to another woman.

Several months after the initial Dorff *vibratorgate* kissing incident, I was off to Ibiza for some filming. Stephen was coincidently going to be there too. Showbiz Simon was with me, as he would be for most of my adventures over the years.

The opening scenes for my Ibiza OK! TV special were to be filmed at the Ocean Beach Club. The beach club wasn't just party central it was the hub of world party culture, the hub of hubs. I was going to see Stephen that night, but first we had filming to do. Which brings up the question:

How many bikinis can a woman wear in a day?

Which would be a totally ridiculous question to ask of course as the answer would be 1.2 million if we had the chance.

But on this occasion, I had to change every hour or so to make it appear that I had been over there for a few days. The younger ravers must have thought 'bloody sad cow' as I kept appearing in a new bikini. Or more likely they probably didn't even have a thought as the drink flowed and the music turned more and more into unfathomable rave.

I had the problem in the afternoon of telling Showbiz Simon, because of Stephen, we would a) not be going out to dinner and b) the filming schedule would be flexible from now on. He protested, but when his back was turned I blew him out like a candle in the wind and trotted off in my heels to the amazing hotel Stephen was staying in.

As I approached his room in a fit of nervous panic, the nagging doubts that started in London came flooding back to me. He was being full on and what was I getting myself into? It was one of those moments where you have two angels on different shoulders, the bad angel going "Yeah go on enjoy the attention honey" and the good one saying "be careful and do you really need this grief in your life?" But when he opened the hotel room door having just come out of the shower, wearing just a small white towel with the body of Zeus, as occasional drips of water ran down his torso, the bad guardian angel punched the good one in the gob and I was all his for the next 3 hours.

I'm not even sure we said hello to each other as the wildness that had started in the suite of all suite's bathroom continued to, well, a wilder level. Lampshades went everywhere, it was edgy, passionate, dangerous and it was a strong 7.5 on the naughty scale, with occasional glimpses of an 8 and we never got below a 6.5.

Halfway through and still no need whatsoever for anything battery operated, my phone started to continually ring and bleep.

"You have to film the links!" said the outraged Showbiz Simon when I finally managed to take a glance at my phone messages. The professionalism that does exist beneath the *outside* me, finally dragged myself away from Torso man's room to Lineakers' bar, owned by Gary's brother Wayne, to talk Simon out of the need to film any links at all.

I turned up there with my hair in the now, I'd like to think fashionable, Tornado style and Showbiz took one disgusted look at me and uttered the immortal Shakespearean phrase, carved from the opening scene of Henry IV part one:

"You f****** s***, what have you been up to?" knowing of course full well what I had been up to.

"Nothing, nothing my darling" replied the innocent TV presenter as she poured champagne down her throat in an attempt to wake up from both the early start and the 7.5 naughty scale activities. I presume we did the links though because I found myself in my hotel room some hours later with no time to spare. The flight back home was due to take off in 70 minutes time. OK! magazine would not be happy AT ALL if we didn't get back to London on schedule.

"Shit, damn, bugger it" I lectured myself as I shoved my clothes into the case. "Why did I take all those bikinis" I wailed as I jumped up and down on the suitcase, finally shutting it in a bottom manoeuvre that only women really know how to perform.

But that turned out to be the easy part. We got outside and disaster stared us in the Iberian face.

"No cabs. No cabs. There are no cabs!" I wailed as I ran around like an hysterical crazy lady, because of course that always works. When I realised it did not, as it never does, I saw a couple of guys in a clapped out old Cadillac parked across the road.

Getting my best flirty voice ready, I walked up to them hips swaying and purred:

"We are going to miss our flight darling, please, please (me oh yeah) could you take us to the airport, we will pay you well of course." And they agreed to. Immediately. Seeing this as a triumph and not at all suspicious, I called over Showbiz and off we went suitcases on our laps in the back.

The journey started rather leisurely it has to be said. Simon pleaded with them "Go faster! Go faster!" but it was then I started to notice a strange smell, a familiar strange smell.

"Go faster!" Simon shouted again, in total panic about what our terrifying friend Richard Desmond boss of OK! would do to us if we were late. To put it into context, there are just 3 people in the world you really don't mess with.

President Putin, your mother-in-law and Richard Desmond.

Then I noticed that the guy in the passenger seat had a brown paper bag in his hand and had started breathing deeply into it. Oh dear I thought, he has a bit of asthma and needs to calm down. He must be terrified of Richard Desmond too. I was just going to offer up some sympathy to him when I realised what that familiar smell actually was.

Glue.

And just as that dawned on me, the passenger seat man handed the brown bag to the driver who stuck his hooter in there, and sniffed the glue like he was the champion of the world glue sniffer.

"Go slower!" Simon shouted in a herculean sudden change of mind as he too realised what was going on up front.

"Hey, don't worry man we are getting you there by a secret route" says Glue man 1 with Glue man 2 nodding his agreement in a chemically high haze of wonderment.

As we headed into the depths of the secret route it suddenly became a weird secret route too, with no other cars around us. Paranoia set in fast.

"We are going to die! We are going to die! They are going to kill us we are all going to diiiiiiiiiiiiiiiiie!" squealed Showbiz in a high-pitched voice, unusual even for him.

If at that moment he had been outside of the car he would have been running around like Benny Hill with his arms flailing about, screaming "We are going to diiiiiiiiiiiiiiiie!" over and over again, it was that dramatic.

"Hey don't worry man, relax it's the quick route" says Glue man 1 with Glue man 2 once again nodding his agreement in a chemically high haze of wonderment. They were a great double act were those glue boys, they could have put on a show at the London Palladium.

It's only looking back now I realise that we were rudely never offered any sniff of the glue. I'm not sure what the glue etiquette is though? If you open a bag of crisps in front of your friends you would probably say "Want one honey?" but a glue sniffer doesn't have the same manners evidently. Shameful.

Simon, now coming to the realisation that sobbing "We are going to diiiiiiiiiiiiiiiiiiiiiiiiiiiiiie" ten times doesn't actually save you, started instead to recite prayers both to himself and to the Lord Almighty, presumably. The glueboys didn't join in, it wasn't part of their normal routine. I took that up a level myself and started to repent my sins, but realised I probably didn't have the time to repent them all. I wasn't about to ask them to go the long way to the 'airport' if indeed that is where we were headed, so I said goodbye to God and throwing eternal salvation out of the window, did the more sensible thing and searched my bag for any small bottle of vodka instead.

As the drama continued in the back seats, Glue 1 and Glue 2 were fairly oblivious to the whole thing which was no doubt because they had half a ton of glue up their nozzers. Then, to add more farce to the farce, right on queue, enter stage left, Stephen Dorff who started his daily text routine to me. *"You don't text me, you have forgotten about me"* read the message and I almost replied *"errr yep that would be right darling as I have been kidnapped and am being driven to the depths of hell"*, but as that would have taken some explaining and time was pressing, I just threw the phone into my bag and focused on the major problem at hand.

Which wasn't the glueboys, but Simon's hysterics.

"We are being driven into the woods, the woooooooooooooods!!!" Simon screamed "We are all going to diiiiiiiiiiiiiiiiiiiiiiie" exaggerating somewhat again in his desperation as we had only passed a small tree on its own, which is probably not what the Oxford English dictionary would define as a 'wood'. But before we could confirm if this did in fact mean we would 'diiiiiiiiiiiiiiiie', a modern day miracle in line with anything written in the Bible appeared, and took its form as a plane. A low flying plane. A low flying plane meant an airport. An airport meant rescue from a fate worse than death in the one tree woods by two glue sniffers pretending to be a west end showbiz double act.

The car stopped outside the airport terminal and we were just about to jump out when we realised the car had a child lock on it. Simon tried to kick it open, knee it open actually, in a pathetic attempt at escape but we need not have worried at all. The glueboys simply ambled around the side of the car and opened the door for us. Because they were actually nice druggies all along with a genuine secret route to get us to the airport quicker.

And to my utter shame reflecting back now, we never paid them anything.

No cash, no pritt stick, no superglue, nothing.

We ran into the airport and didn't even say thank you either. They were of course by that stage so high that if they had been planning to attack us in the one tree wood, it would have been easy to make our escape anyway by simply kicking them in the goolies and legging it.

Safely inside the airport terminal, our drama continued though. To a whole new level of farce.

Showbiz rushed to the check-in counter as I ambled gracefully behind him, barged his way to the front of the queue by flailing his arms around like an hysterical helicopter, and just about managed to splutter out to a startled Spanish lady behind the desk:

"Kidnapped… glue… woods… Withington… Cundy."

She ignored him totally as he was clearly an Englishman who had been out in the midday sun too much and got straight to the point:

"Arse you chekhim in Señor?" she enquired in pigeon English.

Simon was still hyperventilating from the near death glue experience, but in-between deep breaths he managed to splutter out… "My… God… yes" handing both our passports to her.

"Zo Señor, chekin with a Cunty, yes?" observed the Spanish lady in even worse pigeon English.

Which she said just as I arrived at the desk counter.

"Blimey that's a bit of a harsh thing to say about me" I muttered to Simon.

The check-in counter lady stared at the passports again and looked up:

"Yew Señorita arse Cunty... yes... Ms EL Cunty?"

Yep that's right. I'm a Cunty, Ms LCunty, Missile Cunty, arse Cunty, El Cunty and I can be El Sid too if you want me to be.

"Fuck it let's get the next flight out" concluded Showbiz and I didn't disagree with him.

So, we missed the flight, endured an 8 hour wait on standby but we were still alive at least. Showbiz edited the footage at the airport and OK! TV got what they wanted. Richard Desmond never did know what it took for us to get that film to him, and my old friend at OK!, Mark Moody, would have been so proud of me.

Meanwhile Stephen Dorff and I continued our sex text fest. But the messages had dropped to a 5 on the naughty scale and had increased to a 10 on the annoying scale.

"You don't reply, you are forgetting about me" he reminded me yet again. Our trouble ladies is we WANT attention until we actually GET attention. Then it just becomes annoying. *"You don't love me, you don't want me"* came the next wave from Stephen.

And he was right, I didn't.

It was obvious it was going nowhere but he did fly over for another attempt at love, staying at the Mayfair hotel in London. It was just as he arrived and had started to text all the above again, that it suddenly hit me. I had just been told that Mickey Rourke didn't like him and Mickey likes everyone. A man who sleeps with 14 girls in one night probably does like everyone by definition though. But he didn't like Dorff. And therefore my bad vibe feelings about him were probably right. I had been interviewing Denzel Washington in London and the first thing Stephen asked me when I saw him at the Mayfair hotel later was:

"Did you f*** him? You did, didn't you?! I can smell aftershave on you!"

Now it would be pretty impossible in the 20 minute time frame allotted to me to interview Denzel, shag him behind the make-up area and finish before the journalist from the Times turned up for their go (at interviewing, not shagging), but logic and possessiveness are not an intellectual match made in lover's heaven. He had become an angry man and his vibe was getting worse.

I did see him again though in Malibu and had to be saved by Showbiz Simon who was there filming the Oscars with me. Stephen's beach house was magnificent but the conversation was very deep mainly about his mother, and it got to the point where as often as I could I would be texting Simon saying *"Where are you, where are you?"* Despite a brief interlude of a naughty scale 6.8 session it got even weirder with Dorff and he started to say things like:

"You are not leaving me again!" in such a forceful way that even though I wasn't scared, I was very uncomfortable to say the least.

But then Saviour Showbiz rings the front doorbell, comes in and diffuses the whole situation by being as camp as he could be with a "Chop chop, hurry up now little lady we have work to do" routine which stunned Dorff into such silence that we made our getaway quite easily in the end.

The final Dorff Cundy show was held in Claridges where he bolted the door closed after I had entered into his room, giving me the same "You are not leaving" Malibu style routine. That was enough for me and despite a few texts exchanged afterwards, we parted company. I saw him for the last time at the Chiltern Firehouse some months later where we just looked through each other, me managing a simple small nod to him in recognition of the past.

I liked Stephen but he had a complex character and you don't need that in your life after a marriage breakdown.

But he was and still is such a talent.

Gerard Butler

It was widely reported in 2014 that I was seeing Gerard Butler, the Scottish star of numerous Hollywood films including 300. I was with Ross King and a couple of my girlfriends in Chiltern Firehouse and he happened to join us for dinner one night. He seemed just a normal guy, no Hollywood about him at all, no airs or graces, but there was no doubt he was a rough man's man.

We got on really well but were constantly interrupted by ladies coming over to say hello to him, he just didn't get a moments peace. And I'm not sure he knew any of them, they just migrated to him. One strange lady came in with a dog and asked if she could leave it in his room for a while and could he take it up there now and she would go with him. It was at this moment I stepped in and jumped on his knee pretending he was mine. And as I was there it seemed rude not to have a quick kiss so that is what we did.

We had a drink at Chiltern again shortly afterwards but nothing happened, and then I saw him finally at a theatre show when he playfully flicked my bum as he walked past. Let me tell you he has the manliest flick ever, my bottom ached for hours.

There may have been something between us but with the problems I had previously with men who are loved by other women, I thought best not pursue as trouble would undoubtedly follow.

Al Pacino

It was 2014 and my friend Gerry owned a restaurant in Mayfair called Gigi's. He wanted some PR work done to boost recognition for it and so called me up. I arranged some guests to go there for London fashion week but that wasn't quite what he wanted and said we need a big name next time.

I knew many people in the theatre industry and one of them had arranged a 'One night only with Al Pacino' show and he wanted to know where they could go to dinner afterwards and not pay anything for their pleasure. I immediately thought of Gigi's and I got one excited owner happy when I reported back I had secured Al for a night. I felt it best I packed the table with some ladies, so I asked Anthea Turner and Pascal Craymer along too, and then arranged for the celebrity pap Andy Barnes to take some exclusive pics inside during the night to get Gerry maximum coverage. Pascal I thought especially could be a good one as she had previously kept calling him Al Cappuccino on TV and it would liven things up if she still couldn't recall his name. I'm mischievous like that darlings as you have probably worked out by now.

Andy the pap had this show at that time he was part of on TV called Oxford Street Revealed. It was on BBC1 and he brought them along so there was a film crew that night too in the restaurant.

But with a few minutes to go before Pacino arrived I looked out of the window and what I saw freaked me out. Storming outside I found Andy and said to him:

"What are you doing, he isn't going to like this!" as the one pap rule I had arranged as part of the deal with Pacino's manager turned into the 20 pap rule outside. And all just as Al was due to arrive. It looked like a mass celebrity event and not the private intimate thing we had planned.

Gerry, the restaurant owner, was however truly ecstatic. He hadn't reached the stage yet of running around screaming "I'm rich, I'm rich!" but he was getting close to it.

But there was obviously Italian movie star trouble coming so I took Pascal and her big knockers with me to the front door to distract Al when he arrived. They weren't quite big enough to hide 20 paparazzi but it was worth giving it a go. Pacino duly pulled up in a black car and immediately pulled away again to drive around the block. His tour promoter Rocco jumped out though and came steaming over shouting:

"This is a fucking fuck up Lizzie!"

I got the drift.

In fairness it did look like The Cannes film festival outside as Rocco and I negotiated the terms of Pacino's arrival.

"What have you done, what's happening!" he screeched.

"You have to come in now it's all complimentary" I reminded him "and Al must be hungry. Come on one photo outside then come in to eat."

It was like I was at the United Nations.

What they didn't know though is that Denise Welch's husband, Lincoln Townley the artist had been painting a picture of Pacino for some time and they were going to surprise him during the meal by presenting it to him. He had taken forever doing it as he was a big hero of his. It was simply an amazing painting. Or at least that's what I thought.

Al was finally persuaded to come in but was absolutely seething. SEETHING! He was one very unhappy chappy, and even though I wasn't to blame, I was the obvious point of blame.

To make matters worse the film crew were everywhere inside and Al's mood went from seething to, if you look at me I will fuck you up seething. But despite the mayhem going on around him, Al was hungry so he carried on eating. That was until they decided it would be a good time to present him with the Townley painting and Townley himself was going to do that in person. In the presentation party came and out the presentation party went, just like that, which may have had something to do with Al looking at the painting for a split second and in total disgust stating:

"No… nah… don't want that" and sat down to carry on eating his pasta arrabbiata.

Bearing in mind some of Townley's works can sell for £1m, I thought that was a brave "Nah don't want that" thing to say at the time if I'm honest. I felt like creeping up to Pacino and whispering "Al, can you say it's great and then bung it to me outside as you leave."

They tried the presentation again later but that didn't work either. Al wasn't having it. Literally. But he was having his meatballs which had just arrived.

His rudeness got the back-up of most people there but especially one of the fellow guests. Anthea Turner aka The Turner. Don't mess with The Turner when she is on one let me tell you. Anthea bounded up to the BBC cameras and said:

"I'm going to tell you about Pacino. I think it's abysmal, so rude, so rude! Al Pacino couldn't give you 30 seconds, yet how long does a movie last for??"

All hell was breaking loose around Pacino, it was like a scene from the muppets, with rows between everyone and all the time Al is still just eating. His panna cotta had arrived so that was why he wasn't stopping. Italians like their food darlings. He could hear it all happening around him, he frankly just didn't give a shit. Which is kind of cool really. Though not to the artist who went on camera with *Andy the pap* at that very moment:

"That's not good is it, God, think he could have been a little bit more polite" said Andy.

And a shocked Townley could only sigh and mutter to the BBC cameras:

"Yeah" as he stood with the £1m painting that Pacino didn't want (but which Cunders and her ebay account definitely did).

What did I do through all of this rowing and mayhem? Just smiled continuously which is the only way I know how to deal with most problems really. I went from row to row just smiling.

As soon as Pacino's dessert spoon hit his empty plate that night, he was gone with Andy the pap chasing after him to get his picture and Townley the artist running after him to get his recognition, which Pacino eventually relented to by having a photo with the £1m painting he didn't want. I still wanted it though and was plotting a secret heist to stuff it down my bra like I always did with any contraband.

It is a shame that everyone there didn't see Al's charming side that night, but I have during the 4 or 5 times after that I've met him. He is a terrific guy. It was unfortunately just a perfect storm of moody Al that night but he had at least remained in the restaurant eating for 2 hours and Gerry the owner was one happy paying customer for me.

Liza Minelli

I had to interview Liza for OK! TV but when I told her that I was a very good friend of her ex-husband David Gest, it went down like a Hollywood lead balloon. She told me she detested him, that he was the worst thing that had ever happened to her in her entire life and basically - bugger off Lizzie and don't come back.

Not one to ever give up, I disagreed and by some miracle she said to me "Ok let's have a drink and you can try and persuade me."

Which incredibly I tried to do.

Because I thought her ex-husband was a wonderful man and still do.

I first met David when I was filming in a Piccadilly hotel in 2011. You couldn't miss him that day, he had sprayed his hair all red, which wasn't for *show*, he apparently often woke up and did crazy things like that. He stopped me as I was walking past him and said (to someone who was a complete stranger at this point remember) that "I was related to his aunt."

I was so convinced I called up my mum to ask her, but of course he was winding me up, which continued throughout all the time that I knew him. He was simply just like that. Totally hilarious though with it.

We kept in touch over the years and in early 2016 he told me he wanted to do more TV work, so I introduced him to my agent

Vickie White. Within weeks she had got him onto Celebrity Big Brother.

He called me when he heard the news saying he wasn't sure but I was adamant.

"Hey look, you are such a funny guy, people will love you, your funny stories and mannerisms – you have to do it."

He almost pulled out before it started though. He kept telling me "This show would be the death of me." I remember saying often in reply "To stop being so dramatic" and "he would be just great" but on Celebrity Big Brother he was ill a lot of the time during the recording, and he was more poorly than I knew or could ever imagine when he went in there.

On the opening night of Big Brother in early 2016 Vickie and I both turned up to make sure he actually did go in. David was very nervous which I think was real and not him acting like usual. There was definitely a 'will he, won't he' half an hour when you could have flicked a coin either way. He still kept saying "This will be the death of me" time and time again, but then suddenly he was gone and we watched from the green room as the door into the house shut live behind him on TV.

Vickie and I sighed the biggest collective sigh of relief ever and then went to have a massive drink, watching the opening shots from inside the house.

"Job done, see you in a few weeks David, good luck."

I was dozing off later that night in a dozy, sleepy, lovely, dozy, sleepy kind of way when I heard beep, beep beep as text after text came through well past midnight.

Now it's at this point readers where you think two possible things.

Who the bloody hell is being so inconsiderate that they would text me this late?

or,

Someone is in trouble and needs my help.

What you then do is restlessly turn from side to side in bed, your mind battling against both options until you finally convince yourself it's a thoughtless friend, as anyone in trouble would surely call. But then in a John Cleese Basil Fawlty moment, 10 seconds later you shout to yourself in your mind "Right! Bugger it!" and lean across to get your phone off the bedside table to double check no one had suddenly fallen into the Lion's pit in Regents Park Zoo at 2am in the morning and needed me to rescue them.

The texts were from David. He was both an inconsiderate friend and in trouble needing my help, which only he could ever be really. He had apparently, and quite literally, shoved a phone up his arse and smuggled it into the house, past the very tight security.

And that very same phone was now being used to text me.

My first thought was I bloody well hoped he had washed it. And I mean all parts of it not just a quick wipe with a bit of loo roll, but a deep clean into every tiny bit of that phone with anti-bacterial solution and a tooth pick.

My second thought was how was he going to explain this when he got out and his headphone jack didn't work?

"Hello Vodafone, it's Mr Gest here, my speaker doesn't seem to work?"

"Ah Mr Gest, don't worry you are covered by our repair warranty, just bring it into store."

"Can't I just have a new one?"

"No, we will fix it, don't worry we cover all types of repair. We have seen everything before which causes this problem."

"Err, I don't think you have mate" he would reply, hanging up before slinging his phone into the Thames and heading off to the O2 shop down Oxford Street to get both a new phone and number.

His first secret text to me that Big Brother opening night went:

"Lizzie I don't like the people."

followed by

"Help."

"I need my own room."

"Tell Vickie."

With simply no mention of cleaning at all.

I just couldn't believe it. Now darlings I've shoved my phone down my bra a few times before I have to confess to get past security at a TV studio, not to suddenly become a 48DD but simply to get over the 'no photos allowed' rule studio's selfishly adopt to protect the privacy of their stars. David though had uber phone obsession the like of which I had never seen before.

And frankly darlings, without the bacterial wipes being used first, I didn't want to see it either.

In this situation do you admire him, or wonder how much of an effort it was to get the phone in and back out again? How long had it been up there? When I was with him an hour before he entered the house, he didn't appear discomforted in anyway. No moving up and down on his feet, no grabbing hold of his tummy in pain, not one whispered sentence to me of "Jesus my bum hurts Lizzie as it's got an iPhone 6 shoved up it." Nothing.

I didn't text him back that night. I was worried he would get found out and I didn't want to compromise Vickie either.

The press coverage would have been huge though if I had told anyone, no doubt ranging from:

'Cundy forces Gest to shove an iPhone where the sun doesn't shine as she needs attention at all times from her friends.'

to

'Gest shows the way in the economic slowdown as he tries to use all the inclusive texts allowed in his Vodafone monthly package.'

He text me over the next few days again but then the obvious happened. He had tried to bring a charger with him but he couldn't squeeze it into the designated smuggling area so he ran out of battery. A basic schoolboy error therefore I would say.

But that was him. Totally mad. But with a heart of gold. Over the years he would call me up for sometimes hours at night, either doing funny voices where I had no idea it was him or just to give advice, telling me who to trust and who to love in the business we were both in. His advice was always good and always right.

He would relive his Michael Jackson days to me often (he was his manager for a period of time). They went back a long way and he told me he was like a brother to him. It seemed that they both had the same sense of mischief and once, when Michael was staying in London, they both concocted a plan to get on the front page of The

Sun by putting a big plaster onto Michael's nose and all to get the headline *'Jackson has had so much surgery even his nose is falling off.'* Which is exactly what did happen the very next morning after Jackson was papped like that the previous night.

Sadly, very sadly, David died a few months after coming out of Celebrity Big Brother.

Just before he passed away he was planning to do a big Motown tour and call it 'The David Gest I'm not Dead' tour. I told him I didn't like the title, it had such bad karma, it was scary but he had such a funny sense of humour that he loved it, and was adamant that he wanted that as the name. He even asked for my son Josh to work on the tour to give him some experience. He was that nice.

We were due to meet and chat about it all one day at his hotel in Canary Wharf but that morning I got the call that he had been found dead in his room, dying of a heart attack. I was one of the last people to talk to him before he passed away. I was so shocked and upset. I had lost a friend who had my back at all times and who I know truly cared about me. And that type of friend is always so very, very, hard to find.

He was one of life's eccentrics sure, but he was also one of life's really good guys.

And what about my drink with Liza Minneli? Well I tried to convince her about David during it but at the end of our chat she just simply said the next time she ever spoke to him "Would be through a medium."

She hated him that much.

Lionel Richie

I was running late one day in 2012, no surprise there you cry, trying to find a space to park my car. Most of my usual secret haunts were full so I thought I would try The Dorchester where the valet guys knew me well. I whizzed around Park Lane towards the hotel, but my whizzing was too fast as just as I was about to finish parking the car there I suddenly heard a "bang! bang!" on the top of my car roof.

The porters were whacking it and very hard.

I pulled down the window and said to them grumpily "What's up, why are you doing that, I can park a car you know?!!"

One of the them looked at me, sighed, and replied:

"I know that Lizzie but you have just reversed over Lionel Richie's foot."

How do you respond to that?! Not knowing if he was joking or not I jumped out and there he was.

Mr Lionel Richie.

"My God I'm so sorry" I said to him despair growing by the second "I didn't hurt you did I?"

"Well, you nipped my big foot but luckily it's just my foot and not my voice as I'm performing tonight."

In typical Cundy style, this then turned into a chat between us and an invite from him for me to come to his show 'An audience with' which was being filmed by ITV that very night. I duly did go, weirdly hooking up with my hairdresser who had just started to see his assistant.

We went backstage after the stunning show to see him and he was just the loveliest and kindest man. He was still hyped up from the show though so we quickly decided to carry on the chat and headed to the Mandarin Oriental in Knightsbridge.

Everyone was of course then looking at Lionel sat at the bar and despite our best attempts at hiding in a corner section of it, wave after wave of people kept coming over to pay homage to him.

"Ahhh, you helped my marriage with 3 times a lady."

"We had our last dance at our wedding to Hello."

"Can we have a selfie Mr Richie?"

The fans said as they came over, and now repeat that times 10 to get a sense of what was happening that night.

In the end he started saying to people "Get yourself a drink at the bar on me and I will be over soon" so we could actually talk, but then it very quickly looked like hundreds of people were at the bar and the bar bill just kept clicking up and up.

After a while I had to leave as I had TV filming early the next day so he asked for the bill, but when it came he realised in his panic to escape quickly from the show he had left his wallet in the dressing room at the ITV studio's.

Yikes!!

The bar staff didn't believe the old "Sorry I have left my wallet at home" line they had heard a thousand times and even Lionel Richie's IOU wasn't good enough apparently in London. So I offered to pay for him, then realising of course that half of London had been pouring cocktails and vodka down their throats because of Lionel's generosity and would my card have enough limit?

As I waited for the card machine to confirm *payment ok* I wondered what would we do if it did get declined? I settled on the plan of me walking casually back to him, looking over my shoulder and then shouting "Right Lionel, leg it!" as we did a runner out the door towards Hyde Park.

The next day I woke up and never were the words "Hello, is it me you're looking for?" more appropriate as "Yes Lionel I am, could I be repaid for the biggest bar bill in London last night please."

The supreme gentleman that he was, he gave it back to me of course and we stayed in touch and texted. One day he even phoned me when I was having a curry in my local Indian restaurant and sang the 'Hello' song to me which I put on loud speaker and the whole of the restaurant were treated to it.

I now have free curry for life!

Relationships

"Lizzie is simply a good person. She is outgoing, witty and always has a great sense of humour. She is always full of life, has comedic skills, and is a great mediator especially when helping people with problems and with life in general. She is without fail the best person to get you a ticket for any showbiz event.

Lizzie doesn't really have any downfalls, but if pushed I would say that she has a tendency to be late and can be a little disorganised. Mostly late, in fact.

I have known her for four years now and she always makes me laugh. The last time we went to Strictly Come Dancing, she actually hid her phone in her bra, which of course security usually find, she did the very same thing at the recent X Factor final. I would say that she is more obsessed with her phone, than with any man, although naturally we would all like her to find true love. I think that she could easily be with a man that is not connected with show business.

She is addicted to the lifestyle, not to the fame I would say, and I do think that she would miss it if she wasn't part of it.

Her look is now developing into something I have been encouraging for some time. She is always putting a caricature of herself out there, but is incredibly articulate, speaks to everyone, and I consider it to be a gift to be so welcoming. She makes everyone that she meets feel important and I think her story is one of 'I will survive'.

When Lizzie reads derogatory stories written about her, she tries not to let these affect her. She has an amazing ability to remain mentally strong and to carry on regardless. This naturally is a great credit to her.

I met Lizzie at Royal Ascot, and as soon as we met, we hit it off instantly. Her friendly, easy- going nature, and the fact that we connected on many levels including our humour, made us destined to become great friends. Lizzie was also a model, of course, and I am the owner of a model agency."

Paul Cavaliar - Managing Director Nevs Model agency

W hat am I searching for in a man? If you are a single lady now what are you searching for? If you are with someone now, are you searching for something else?

Men are frustrating. Love is frustrating. Do we need love? I have the love of my friends and family and that is uncomplicated love. How you fall out of love with someone though is difficult to understand really, but it happens all the time.

I have been thinking a lot about it all since my time on Shirley Valentine in the summer of 2018. The problem is if you start to open yourself up to a camera as I did on that show about love, the press will then have a field day.

'My Shirley Valentine Summer is a festival of self-loathing.' The Guardian wrote about it.

'These women carry their emotional baggage alongside their designer suitcases. They expose the vulnerable side of the tabloid tales, the women scorned that carry on quietly after the scorching spotlight has been dimmed. Theirs is the empty psychological hangover suffered after their private lives have been split open and rummaged around in like an errant bin bag by the public until another distraction arrives.'

Which translated means we shouldn't really ever analyse love. But we do all the time of course.

Men are often like little boys. Or dogs. Give them a treat once in a while and generally they are happy in their man world. A man will not shower you with the same daily affection we shower them with. But when they say I love you it has an effect maybe we don't give them enough credit for.

I like being with a man. I like someone who is funny, exciting, a bit naughty, usually tall, usually dark and to fast track to the finer details,

I don't really care about hairs on the chest or not. I suppose I would prefer a Sean Connery to a Roger Moore. Brains are good. I don't like dull men, quiet men who are hard work, I like generosity and a bit of mischief. I like looking after men, I like sometimes being a *mother* to them but I'm strongly also in favour of women's rights.

I am old-fashioned with regards dating and men's manners towards woman in general though. On a first date I believe a man should be expected to pay the bill, it's not about the money it's about the principle. If a guy asks you out then it's nice if he also then treats you as part of that evening.

But my God I got hammered on a TV show once when I dared to mention that, one paper reporting:

'Lizzie Cundy was slammed by This Morning viewers earlier today for insisting a man should always pay on a first date.'

'The ITV Daytime show were doing a feature on the age-old debate which sparked outrage after a recent episode of the Channel 4 series First Dates in which the man lost his rag when his date Mary wouldn't split the bill.'

'The presenter - who is known for being a socialite and former WAG of footballer Jason Cundy - came under immediate fire after saying that she things that every woman - if they're honest - wants to be treated, especially on a first date. Viewers took offence, saying Cundy was 'stuck in the dark ages.''

But I stand by what I said then. I went on a date once and at the end it was the absolute height of embarrassment. He started to quibble the bill with me at the end.

"Ok Lizzie, you had a starter, so that's £7.67 and then a steak bringing it to £20.95, and I would say you drank more of that bottle of wine than me so I'm going to allocate 67% to you" and on and on he went. When he got his calculator to do the final reconciliation, I just got up, paid the bill myself and left.

I like old-fashioned manners in a man. I was in a meeting recently and a guy got up and opened the door for a lady. She immediately snapped at him:

"I can open the door myself thank you" and then the man had to call his HR department to explain in case he got accused of sexual discrimination, and all because he hadn't opened the door to a man ever.

Should a woman be a Victorian wife or a modern day wife? Did I do the wrong or right thing looking after and supporting a sportsman in the way I did? For his health and recovery of course I did what any person should do, but should I have been so subservient generally around him, which in fact ultimately cost me my marriage when I couldn't maintain the same *subservient* level I was at before. But I was happy to do that at that time and if I'm honest I loved doing it as I saw that his career could fly and therefore it would benefit all of us. It became too familiar to him though and familiarity breeds contempt when something someone is so used to just isn't there anymore.

I cared for Jason during our marriage on all levels and showed that in many ways. When he got injured once playing for Ipswich, where he was captain, I was so worried he would be out for a year that when I happened to be at the ground one day, and the Chairman David Sheepshanks called me up to his office to have a chat, I went with the intention of seeking information about his contract. I was terrified that his dreams may end soon. I went into Sheepshanks office and saw Jason's picture was hanging proudly behind him, which convinced me he was still very much in his plans and the plans for club.

As I came out of the office I bumped into Steve Sedgley, at that time an Ipswich player, and said how pleased I was as the picture was there which must mean things would be ok.

Until that is Steve replied, "Lizzie the chairman has a photo of all the players and changes them depending what person is invited in to see him!"

Despite that, or indeed because of that, I believe strongly in women's rights and women's equality and any form of discrimination is simply appalling. And yet some will label me as encouraging it all by being an old-fashioned wife for many years. But everyone has the right to feel comfortable in whatever they believe is best and I believed that was best at that time.

Looking back, I still think it was the right thing to do.

I like the excitement of meeting someone new for the first time. The butterflies. But it's so easy for people now, there were no mobile phones back when I was growing up. Remember those times? You had to work at your relationship then, now you can go into a pub, fast track the dating by just pressing a button on Tinder and someone appears by your side. You could probably go the whole evening without even talking to someone.

I suppose I go for dangerous men. I believe I can change them despite their track record and though it's hard to admit it to yourself, I am naïve about that. I believe that the good exists in everyone.

Celebrity Lizzie is actually vulnerable Lizzie.

But anyone dating me comes with the problem that I have a huge social life. I am a social butterfly so is it possible for me to meet anyone who society would define as 'normal' and not a celebrity? I'd like to think I could date someone like that, but I haven't really tested the theory. When you have met Madonna, George Michael, Prince, Simon Cowell, Leonardo DiCaprio, Al Pacino, God knows how many professional sports stars, and been on many TV shows for the last ten years then it's hard to be 'normal' in any sense and I have been in that celebrity world since I was born.

I long for normality but am petrified at the very thought of it.

Do I search now for love? No, I don't. I have enough affection in my life, but I search for companionship and there is a difference I think, or you know maybe there isn't. I believe I will be married again and when that time comes, will my life be complete? I have so much to thank God for already that sometimes it seems selfish to want more. But we all deserve to be loved and wanted because it makes us feel special and it brings excitement when we leave the house. We all know how that feels and it feels good, we don't have to deny that we love that emotion.

How would I cope with looking after someone again, washing for them again with that routine of someone always being there night after night? I don't know, but I like to think I could still be good at it, I am not afraid of that. But I am used to driving my own affairs and schedule now and that would be an issue to overcome. I certainly recognise that.

Men seem to cheat. Not all but some. It seems to be in their DNA to want to. They don't seem to have the same logic as ladies to say no. And when a man cheats there is often no logic to who he cheats with. To them it's the thrill of the chase. They think they are pirates so they spurt out one "Ahhh Jim lad" to prove it, and off they trot like Blackbeard to find a new woman to walk the plank with.

The easiest way to stop the problem of cheating is to allow them to cheat. Have an open marriage. But it should work both ways and you watch the reaction of your husband when he gets in, says "What's for dinner?" and you reply "sorry honey there isn't any, I'm off out with Trevor the postman tonight so I've been busy getting ready. No need to wait up for me."

And there is absolutely no logic to them believing they won't get caught either, and the risks they therefore take because of that flawed logic. They really do seem to believe that they will always get given a second chance.

I was at an Oasis concert around 2013 and I recognised the man just in front of me as Grant Bovey, Anthea Turner's Husband. I didn't know either of them at the time and I thought the girl with him that night must have been his daughter, she seemed that young. The next day I was drinking at the Chelsea Harbour Hotel and they were both there but obviously not as father and daughter as they were all over each other. Just like that in public and Grant and Anthea were pretty high profile back then too.

I called my manager at the time to tell her all this as she ironically was Anthea's manager too, and within a few hours our manager had a call from Anthea saying she suspected her husband of cheating. And of course, she was right.

Anthea and I have been close ever since, but this wasn't subtle cheating by Grant Bovey it was in your face I'm untouchable cheating.

When I split up with someone I never seek revenge. The nuns installed a sense of morality in me and I believe karma will come back around if I do a bad thing or if they do a bad thing.

So, I don't need to bother, God is looking after that one for me.

But be careful my darlings. Even though we all play that game with our friends or in our heads of describing our perfect man, that in itself can be flawed. It's a case sometimes of be careful what you wish for.

I will explain why.

Most of us would like our partners to be clever I guess. Brains would be on a lot of lists of the top 10 things we would want in a man. However, it's all very well being clever, but sometimes I don't want 15th century French poetry recited to me when I'm a Celebrity Get Me out of Here is about to start. Sometimes I don't want to do the Times crossword at 11pm in bed, I want to read OK! magazine and dribble over the pictures of Brad Pitt.

Take romance ladies. Oh yes, you all cry we must have that in a man and I wouldn't disagree. But sometimes when you are out for dinner you just want to eat your pasta you don't need 3 violinists playing 'Angels' standing next to you as you do it. In bed I don't really want to hear all the time "My sweet darling can I now make perfect love to you?" sometimes I want to be told "lie down baby I want to **** *** **** out of you." I'm fickle like that!

What about attention! My God, yes, you all cry we want, no insist, our men give that to us. We need that all the time. And we do. But we don't really. When your man doesn't want to leave your side and is stroking your arm all the time it can become a tad annoying especially when he wants to be part of the ladies gang you have, and all you just want is for him to go so you can, well, gossip about him. And attention through new age communication? WhatsApp, texting etc. Lovely to be thought of and to get a few messages throughout the day but when they keep coming at you like the Zulus at Rorke's Drift, you will get so fed up all you want do then is just copy and paste a reply you did previously, and finally resort to just turning your phone off or indeed throwing it into the River Thames.

A successful businessman, now that would be lovely ladies I know you will agree with me. Any successful man is attractive. But if I'm married to one, when he gets home and I ask:

"How was your day darling?"

I'm not really that interested enough to look through his PowerPoint of it examining what happened, and the effect the dollar to the pound had on his earnings per share that morning. And when he starts criticising you because you want to try something new which wasn't in the original 5 year plan he created for the relationship at the start, then this could be the beginning of a problem.

People change in a relationship. You have to recognise this is going to happen. If it starts fairly immediately after meeting, then you probably have the moral high ground to stop the wheel, but after many years people are bound to be different, desires will be different. I was married 23 years and I took my eye off the ball apparently at the end. But didn't I have the right to 'change' after so many years? And it actually wasn't me changing it was the dynamic of the relationship changing.

Confused?

Ok, imagine you are Yoko Ono and have just met John Lennon in the late 1960's. Stay with me darlings there is a point to this. Lennon at the time was an outspoken borderline revolutionist who had been brave enough to proclaim the Beatles were becoming bigger than Jesus Christ, and had sent his OBE back to her Majesty the Queen in protest at some protest.

Now I know this is artistic license (as she didn't feel like this), but say if Yoko had rocked up at that time and thought - whey hey, this will be exciting being with a Beatle and the dangerous one at that, this will be life on the edge for me now.

But in the 70's Lennon decided to spend many years at their home in New York virtually never leaving the apartment to look after their son instead (a true story).

Yoko then tries to get the man she married, as they had only just married, to be, well, like the man she had only just married.

"Don't you want to come out now Mr Beatle the sun is shining in central park" she pleads one day.

"What year is it Yoko?"

"1973."

"Ah, I will wait until 1976 thanks all the same love."

Not what she signed up for!

She has a right to say to Lennon "Oi, you have taken your eye of the ball you are dull." So, if she buggers off with Ringo after that, you would say, fair enough good luck to you. But if after being a revolutionary for 22 years of their marriage he then said I've had enough I'm staying at home for a while, she has to understand people change and that was probably always going to happen as you can't keep up the same pace forever. So, her running off with Ringo then would not be morally acceptable in the law of the love jungle.

I think that's why some men want to cheat as they always want things as they were when you first met them, and a new woman will more than likely give that to them. Until of course she then changes and the hamster wheel comes around again.

Imagine there's no cheating, it's easy if you try.

Finally, in this chapter of men and relationship analysis, I want to end my award-winning thesis by talking about sex. At last you cry out, spill the bloody beans Cunders!! But no darling, I'm not going to give you all a clearer definition of the naughty scale, instead we need to revisit something I mentioned in the opening part of this book.

The Mickey 14 a night.

The reaction to that story from men to Mickey I'm sure would be "Well done, good on you son!" but to a woman is it "wow I wish I was with someone like that, I'm lucky if my man lasts for 14 minutes" or is the lady going to think "what an egotistical male chauvinist pig."

Whichever it is, the Mickey '14 in one night' story does leave a lot of unanswered questions which I shamefully didn't tackle when he told me that at the time in our interview.

Like how did he decide the order? Would number 14 be the best or the worst? When you have dinner, you may leave the best part of the food until last, so is 14 the best mouthful you have saved or just a number to boost, well, the numbers? Did he say to 14 "Hurry up love my waffles are about to arrive" as the sunrise came up or did he stare into 14's eyes and say "you are the one I have had been longing for all my life."

Or is say number 3 the best as he is warmed up by then? Did the ladies know their number order? Or was 14 actually 14 in one go on a steel reinforced bed?

If someone went twice did that count as 1 go or 2 in the 14? If there were twins was that 1 or 2 in the counter? How did he know it was 14 anyway, did he mark them off like he was playing bingo as the ladies left? How did he know their names? Is it like the Queen when the Palace butler whispers in her ear, as the dignities file by which, in Mickey's case it would be a man appearing from under the bed saying "That's Sharon, Mickey" as the next blonde tart walks into *le boudoir*.

And what about the linen? Were the sheets changed after each one? Were the hotel maids on standby outside? And what counts as achieving a number? Do you have to go the whole way or part way? Did he actually orgasm each time?

And when each left, did he have someone take a survey outside so he could improve on the performance he would give with the later numbers?

It could be a multiple choice type survey with a lady using a clipboard:

Tell me Mickey 4…

How would you rate the conversation after sex this evening?
A) He was very loving and attentive.
B) Not bad but seemed to be looking over my shoulder at the door.
C) Terrible with him but good with the maids as they changed the satin sheets after.
D) What conversation, he jumped straight out of bed to watch Match of the Day.

How would you describe the foreplay?
A) Attentive to my needs and made sure I had an equal share of the enjoyment.
B) If foreplay is defined as I did it all, then it was excellent.
C) There was none whatsoever, he said sorry for the delay but it had been a long night and as soon as he could get his knob to rise again, could I jump on board and get it over with quickly as he had a target to reach!

Were the ladies queuing outside the room to get in? Was it like at Disney where you can get a fast pass ticket to go to the front of the queue? When the ladies left, like at Disney, was there a souvenir shop you had to go through to the exit which sold things like tattoos with *I'm one of the Mickey 14* on them or a T-shirt which had *I've been Rourked* on it, or a poster which printed the song words *Oh, Mickey you're so fine, you're so fine you blow my mind, hey Mickey.*

It's all so confusing isn't it darlings, love and relationships.

But that, no doubt, is why it is also so exciting.

Carry on Lizzie

"Lizzie and I met, God, it must be 18 years ago at GMTV where I did her make-up for the show. She's a woman you instantly fall in love with as a friend. Lizzie has such a kind heart and a fun cheeky way about her. She's both a woman's woman and a man's woman.

I think people look at Lizzie Cundy in the papers and on the red carpet and confuse her with someone she's not. She is the first one to help you in your time of need, and goes above and beyond to make sure you're ok. You could call her any time of day or night and she's there for you, a total heart of gold. I think it would take someone very special to turn Lizzie's head.

She's had such a tough time of it, most people have no idea what she's gone through and what she's had to fight for. People see a pretty woman in a nice dress smiling and would say her life is easy, she has no worries like they would have. Little do they know, they couldn't be further from the truth.

Lizzie was born to be in show business, it's her comfortable place as well as being home with her boys.

I'll call her one minute, and she's on TV, next thing you know she's rushing home to sort the boys out, drop James somewhere and then back into London for not just one red carpet or showbiz party, but two or three in the one night. It might look like fun to the outside world, but trust me when I say it's exhausting! She copes well with it though, and is often mischievous and cheeky, that's her personality, full of fun.

I was next to Lizzie on the red carpet one night where she was interviewing the cast at a film premiere. She told me she needed the loo, handed me the mic and asked me to interview the next Hollywood actor who came along. Before I could say 'I haven't seen the movie', she was gone! Thankfully Josh (Lizzie's son) gave me a quick rundown of the storyline before the next actor came along. Luckily, the main character had to wear lots of make-up in the movie, making it easier for me to ask appropriate questions as I'm make-up artist. A few minutes later Lizzie came back laughing. To this day I'm not even sure she went to the loo!"

Helen Hand – make-up artist to Lorraine Kelly and to Lizzie Cundy

My life seems to be one adventure after another where I find myself in all sorts of situations and doing all manner of things I never planned to. It really is like a carry on movie some days, you just simply couldn't make it up. Most of it caused by me blagging my way into some situation or event.

Darlings you don't believe me?

Well read these…

Putin

I was at the Arts Club in Mayfair in the early months of 2015 and had arranged to meet a Russian friend there who was thinking about writing her life story as a possible prelude to a TV series being shown of it in the UK. She was a very rich but hugely likeable socialite, who's focus was on raising money for humanitarian causes and especially those for children's charities.

Her name was Ella Krasner.

We had started a really pleasant chat about how things could work moving forward, when suddenly what can only be described as a larger than life Russian lady came over who didn't wait for any introductions and immediately started talking with Ella in Russian.

After what seemed to be a good couple of minutes of me fiddling with everything I could fiddle with, she suddenly acknowledged my presence. Which was very gracious of her I thought.

"Who is thizzz beautifuuuul laaady zat you hide from me?" she said to Ella about master of disguise Cundy, who was hiding behind a small wine glass on the table. She turned to face me and her huge boobs swung around in a frantic pendulum motion nearly knocking my head off, which let me tell you would have been bloody annoying as I had only just had my hair done!

No matter what Ella or I said, or hinted to her thereafter she just wouldn't leave us alone. To cap it all she then started to develop an unhealthy liking for the red bag I had with me.

I kid you not.

"I love zat red bag" she proclaimed after staring at it for 10 seconds.

Ella and I continued to talk to each other.

A minute later she poked me in the ribs.

"Where is zat red bag from darling?"

Ella shrugged her shoulders, as bemused as I was but managed to whisper to me that "She isn't normally like this."

45 seconds later.

"I zimply adore zaaat red bag Lizzzzzzie."

And by that time, I thought "Do you know what love, you have it!" if that is what it takes for you to leave us alone. So I smiled my Lizzie smile said "Here you are" and actually then handed it over to her.

And without any shame, she actually then took it from me.

Not just that either. She immediately emptied all my stuff out of it as well onto the coffee table, looking at me very disappointingly afterwards it had to be said. Can't think why?

On the table there now appeared a half eaten small bag of cashew nuts, 54p in loose change, a pink lip gloss and a receipt from 2013 for something that was important enough in 2013 for me to keep a receipt for.

"Ahh you are zeee kindest girl, pleaze I just have to tell you zat, pleaze let me have a picture of you" she then said rather demandingly and before I could reply "Yes, no, maybe, my left side is the best, can you put your best filter on it before it goes anywhere my darling, I own the image rights" or "can I have a copy for insta please" she simply snapped away like we were long lost best friends and triumphantly declared that "she would be back zoon" before her, and her mega boobs waltzed triumphantly off into another part of the club.

And I still simply had no idea who she actually was.

"Watch yourself there Lizzie" said Ella when Mrs Red Bag was out of sight, "she is a hard-nosed lady who happens to be very well connected in Russia... if you know what I mean" and to reinforce that point she looked up to the ceiling of the Arts Club and pointed in that direction for more effect. I followed her gaze and her point. She looked up again, knowingly. I looked up again not really knowingly but pretending I definitely was.

"So... she is high up in the Russian clergy then?" I said finally to stop the back and forth look upwards towards God.

Ella put her finger to her lips as if to say "Shhhh" looked around to make sure no one was listening, which would have been correct as clearly no one was, shook her head, looked around again, leaned forward and whispered:

"No... higher than God... Kremlin."

Blimey I thought, I have therefore just made a friend from the KGB which would come in bloody handy if I ever wanted a parking ticket overturned at some point in the future.

Just then KGB Red Bag Lady returned.

"I haz news for you!!" she exclaimed excitedly to me "I have zent your picture to my bezzzt friend and he now loves you!"

"That's ever so sweet darling it really is" I replied to her "but Ella and I have to chat about things, so maybe we could take this up a bit later?"

Mrs Red looked at me. And rather menacingly it had to be said.

"Do yoooooou knowz who my friend is?" she gazed into the eyes of a now little bit scared Lizzie.

Queue a dramatic pause. A very dramatic pause.

"My friend" she triumphantly proclaimed puffing her uber boobs out even more "is Vladimir Putin. I am one of hiz closest friends as I went to school wiz him. He haz now invited you to come to hiz ball in Mossssscow as hiz personal guest."

Wow!

I have to say that news was worth the dramatic pause readers I'm sure you will agree.

"You have to come, he haz perzonally invited you" she lectured me and to prove her point she showed me the text from him on what I assume was the Russian version of mobile phone texting. Better known from the Urals to the Chinese border as WhatsAppski. In fairness the text was all in Russian so she could have been talking about carrots, but the profile picture was definitely him which made the colour leave my face immediately. The most powerful man on earth.

"Gosh, that's really kind thank you so much, but I will have to confirm" I managed to get out of my colourless mouth desperately now in need of lip gloss.

She pointed at me.

Pause for dramatic effect again. Her eyes stared intensely at me.

"You zimply must come!!" was all she said (ordered) as the Putin pimp turned on her heels and strolled purposefully out of the Club, with my red bag over her shoulder and the most powerful man in the world in her WhatsAppski contact list.

I was in full-blown panic mode.

"You have to go there with me" I begged to Ella who then made some lame excuse like "get lost I don't want to" and then rammed home the fact that I had to "you can't say no to Putin as only special people get asked to things like that."

So as *the special one*, aka me apparently, left the Arts Club some time later with 54 pence and some cashew nuts in her coat pocket, lip gloss in her hand and shoving a receipt from 2013 into the bin, a little cheeky smile arrived at the thought of flying into Moscow airport without any sort of Visa or papers.

"WHERE IS YOUR VISA LADY?" the passport control guard would shout at me spitting onto the floor at my feet in total and utter western contempt.

"But I'm here to see Putin my darling" I would reply all innocently back at him.

"Ah, why didn't you say? Then welcome to Russia Mizz Lizzie Cundski, your limo is outside and here is a special vodka for you to enjoy as I escort you myself through baggage and customs so you don't have to waste any more time with these trivial formalities."

In my Lizzie wisdom I thought this trip could be fun. A grand adventure. 'He who dares wins Rodders' and all that. I would be like the Russian spy in a Bond movie, I would dance at a glittering ball overlooking Red Square, I would eat caviar in the Kremlin and depart into the early hours of a cold, but utterly beautiful Moscow day looking like Shirley Bassey with my massive fur hat on.

So, it was rather harsh I thought when no one (literally no one) I asked to come with me on the trip saw it the way I did, preferring the more boring argument of "I would be asking for trouble" and "it could be off to the Siberian Gulag for 5 years hard labour if I said the wrong thing at any time."

Which knowing me my darlings, I would definitely have done.

Boring 1 Adventure 0.

"Sorry" I said to Red Bag KGB lady when I called her up a few days later, "so, so sorry I can't make it, I have plans I just can't get out of" and thankfully she didn't ask what plans were more important than meeting Vladimir Putin, President of all Russia, because I would then have had to explain to her that I was now going out with Anthea Turner that night for a Pizza.

She did though give me a consolation prize instead.

"He is having a special party at ze Russian Embassy in London in a few weeks time and you have to come to zat Lizzzzzzzie."

Which I duly did. Though it was all very dull and over quickly. Like sex with most men really then.

When I arrived I saw him chatting away in the corner with a couple of people as if it were an ordinary drinks party, though it was obvious from the security a few steps away on every side of him in the shadows, that this was not an ordinary person at an ordinary drinks party.

Mrs Red took me over.

"Zis is Lizzie" she nodded very knowingly to him.

"Ah, you didn't make the party" he immediately replied in surprisingly good English and we chatted a little bit more before having a goodbye kiss side to side, a shake of the hands and then it was offski into the London night for Comrade Cundy.

Now hang on you are thinking. And I would reply "I know, I know!"

I feel guilty enough already don't ram it home anymore.

I bottled the request for a selfie with him.

Please forgive me darlings.

Bruno Tonioli

It was late 2016 and I had been given a complimentary trip to the Maldives. As part of that arrangement I would also be bringing my great friend Bruno Tonioli from Strictly Come Dancing with me, so he could judge a ballroom dancing competition. We stayed in a magnificent hotel and Paul our mutual friend came along too.

As we arrived though Bruno went straight to his room. He was jet lagged. As I walked around the resort with Paul we noticed all these posters everywhere of Bruno and the dancing competition but it just made him look like a magician or in fact Paul Daniels to be precise.

Bruno being Bruno would be all Diva if he saw any of those around, so we rushed around ripping them down from trees and anywhere else we found them. People would walk past and we would stand by whistling innocently, then when they were out of sight rip them down and go onto the next. There was even one on the gym wall which I accidentally threw some water over, tore down and shoved it into my bra for safe keeping.

The day arrived for the guests first dance training session in advance of the competition and Bruno decided he didn't want to do it. Still jet lagged and not in a great way anyway he had also been devastated by the news coming through that George Michael had just died. Bruno knew him well having choreographed many of his videos for him.

Thinking fast, which I had years of training on, the hotel would throw us out if we didn't 'perform' so there was only one thing for it. I would pretend I was involved in Strictly and I would do the lessons. Paul went totally white as 30 or so people walked in and I told them I was their instructor.

"Ok let's warm up" said the Lizzie from Strictly Come Dancing you had never heard of, and I started to do my Olivia Newton John 'Let's get physical' routine. Whilst they warmed up, I typed into Google "How the bloody hell do you do the tango?" and worked out a version that may work.

Which essentially was nothing like the tango.

As I started to sound all knowledgeable to my group of dance students, one of the buggers there pipes up that he actually did ballroom dancing and basically implied, quite unfairly I felt, that I was utter rubbish. Which I was but it was still unfair. My immediate comeback to *Mr Know It All* who did know it all was that:

"This was the new modern version of the tango and variety in training was essential for the group if I was to bring out their undoubted talents further. This new dance was going to be in the next series of Strictly so they were bloody lucky basically to have this exclusive, and *Mr Know It All* who did in fact know it all should shut his know it all gob for a bit."

They fell for it big time. It really is no wonder I got out of all that homework at school. And all the time Paul was hanging onto the dance rail for dear life in case he collapsed onto the floor in a heap of laughter.

But my God I gave it my all to them.

"Shoulders back, breathe, feel it, feel it, feel the drama darlings feel the moment."

"Bottoms in, arms up, feel it, work it, live it. LIVE IT!"

I looked up and to my horror the owners had now arrived and were watching the class. But instead of the immediate eviction from the hotel to the YMCA down the street, seeing the look of happiness on the guests faces, they asked Paul and I if we could do it all again in a few days time.

We were that good apparently.

We didn't want to be thrown out into a room that sleeps 28 students who hadn't washed for at least 10 days, so we agreed. I thought I would up my game though, and so how the bloody hell do you do the waltz? was typed into Google the next day with Paul and I trying to make any sense at all of its intricacies. But we winged our way through it in practice with the guests by essentially giving the same mantra, that it was a new version of the waltz.

Left: Another fab interview with my dear friend Simon Cowell.

Below: My stylist Lara Accison and good mate Jean-Bernard Fernandez, Cheryl's ex.

Right: LA fun papers going bonkers. Making it in the States!

Below: Another fun night with Eamonn, Sky News weather girl Naz Ghaffar, Caroline Monk and my good friend Helen Hand.

Lizzie looks great in the States!

SNAPPED UP: Lizzie's caught the eye of NBC

Left: Strictly dancer Kristina Rihanoff and Jessica Knowles.

Right: Helen Hand, good friend and Lorraine Kelly make-up artist, Eammon Holmes at Ross Kings book launch.

Left: Out with the boys at my birthday party. Julien, Jason and the boys!

Right: Nicholas Cowell and my chum Carol.

Below: My great friend actress Susan George, Jo Wood and Simon Withington.

Left: Me and Kristina. I was one of her first friends when she came from Russia to do Strictly.

Below: Having a laugh with Christian Slater.

Right: David Gandy and I at the Scottish Fashion awards.

Left: There are many GMB debates against Piers Morgan, but I adore him.

Right: With Stephen Fry. His parents are good chums with my mum.

Left: Funny headlines.

Below: Great fun with great friends at my birthday with Jo Wood and Julien Macdonald.

Right: Another Caudwell charity event with Jo Wood and Melinda Messenger.

Left: In la-la land... making headlines for the bikini

Right: Joining Nevs models... at the ripe old age of 50.

Left: Nights out with Will.i.am.

Below: Roger Daltrey one of the nicest guys I've met.

Left: With Craig Revel Horwood on Strictly. Who's wearing more make-up?

Below: Filming the pilot for a new make-over show with Anthea Turner, Tonia Buxton and great pal Vickie White.

Left: Siân Lloyd on the set of 'Our Shirley Valentine Summer'.

Below: Actress Patricia Penrose and celebrity chef Aldo Zilli.

Right: Cannes film festival with Mr Louboutin himself!

Below: Me with Jeremy Vine. Who would believe that we would have so much in common!

Left: With Tito Jackson at David Gest's Motown night.

Right: Alex Silver one of the best beauty PR in the UK.

Left: David Furnish at Elton John's bash.

Right: Me and my new found friend Kim Kardashian.

Left: My radio shows are never dull! A python in the Talk Radio studio as I'm broadcasting.

Right: Alex Gerrard and me on a Lipsy clothing night out.

Left: My fave pic of my boys.

Below: Jay my closest non showbiz pal with my son James.

Right: Launching my 'ITV at the Movies' show with Baz Lurmen at the relaunch of Romeo and Juleit. Jason had just left 24 hours before.

Below: Showbiz Simon.

Left: The girls from Shirley Valentine on a night out.

Below: Joy Desmond and me at the Arts Club. She always manages to cheer me up!

Right: The ladies who changed my life, Shirley Valentine booker Stef Alexsander and my friend and manager Vickie White

Left: Old friend Susie Homes. We did the WAG fashion show together that went mental on all the news when the WAGs just hit the headlines.

Right: Actress Naomie Harris in Barbados. She gave Josh some great acting advice.

Left: With Richard Madeley. I had grown up always watching Richard and Judy on 'This Morning'. It was a show I had always wanted to present on.

Below: Petula Clark and Sheryl Howard at David Gest's do.

Right: Me with old time friend and fellow Chelsea fan Jake with bestie Jay at Browns nightclub.

Below: Simon and I together at an interview for This Morning.

Left: With Julie Walters modelling for Women's Aid charity against domestic violence.

Below: Lauren Silverman and I sharing secrets.

Right: Another fun night with Bruno and Paul.

Left: Harry Styles backstage at 'The X Factor'. Funny story here.

Right: Love filming with the This Morning show! I'm good for giggle even if they make me dress as GaGa !

Lizzie Cundy dresses up as LADY GAGA as she sports platinum wig and structured black gown to emulate singer's Oscars look

Left: My two sons. Best mates still to this day. James is a bit more of a live wire than Josh.

Below: Tom Cruise and I after our fun night.

Above: At the National Television Awards 2019.

Finals day arrived and Bruno was going to at last make an appearance. But having spent most of the week sunbathing with 8 bottles of coconut oil poured all over him, he looked like bacon, he was so burnt and frankly walked like bacon too he was that fried.

The show started. The Strictly music started, Bruno livens up until he witnesses the couples dancing and leans over to us saying "I've never seen dancing like that in my life" and for dramatic effect, after 5 seconds more of staring at them with his mouth open, added "ever."

But we got away with it. I always do. One couple who were on the verge of breaking up reignited their love for each other because of the dancing we were told, and I don't know how the owners came to this conclusion, but we were invited back to do the following years show too!

Which we ever so politely declined.

Rugby World Cup

It was during the 2015 Rugby World cup in England that I almost caused a match fixing scandal that would have shocked the world. But before you get carried away that I was part of some far east betting syndicate rigging game, it was caused by lust. And not mine I might add. Well, not all mine.

In this story I can't use this player's proper name but it is all very true none the less. It's complicated don't ask. So, I will call him Leo instead.

Leo was doing really well in that World Cup and I had known him a while. But his schedule during the tournament was very tight and I was busy myself too, though we had been texting in the lead up to the tournament and during it quite a bit. Naughty scale 7, as you asked so nicely. He told me he was single and I believed him, as I always do. But as I write now I don't think he was but I had no idea about that at the time.

I got a text saying he was in London and I must come and see him. Trouble was, I knew this was the night before a mega game for him but he was insistent saying he couldn't get to sleep unless I went to see him.

Seize the moment Cunders, or Carpe Diem Cunders to be cleverly more precise and even though it was quite late, I rocked up to the lobby of his hotel as agreed. I must have been totally insane. It was packed, as of course it would be the night before a massive game and even though I had his room number I was not going to chance it, for mine and his sake. I did a quick u-turn and hurried back to my car, texting him that there were just too many people about and I didn't think it a good idea anymore.

"No, no, I have to see you" he text back *"I will come to you just wait a bit in the car for me."*

Which I did and within 10 minutes there was a knock at the window and in he gets. One of the best rugby players in the world on the eve of a massive match had jumped out of his hotel room 2nd floor window to meet me. And the first thing he said when he got into my car was:

"My God I've hurt my leg, it's killing me."

I was mortified and he was in full panic mode too.

Funnily enough though that didn't stop him kissing me, and when he started to make lots of oooo and ahahh noises I thought, ah ha Cunders you still have it then girl, until I realised the noises he was making related to his leg pain. Which was seemingly getting worse by the minute, so much so, he made his apologies and I watched him hobble in the darkness back to the hotel to get some midnight physio. I have no idea what he said to his coach to explain it, but the next day when he came onto the pitch he was heavily strapped up and I'm watching the game with 10 of my friends thinking "I did that."

His team won though and he played well. I got away with it, as I always do.

Harry Styles

It was the night of the X Factor semi-final in 2012 and I had amazing tickets with backstage passes so I took my boys along with me. I thought it would be great fun, the divorce from Jason had just come through and all 3 of us needed a distraction.

We arrived, went backstage, and all of a sudden my youngest son James, who was just 11 at the time, disappeared. Just like that. The show was being filmed at Fountain Studios in Wembley which was not the biggest place in the world to say the least, so he couldn't have gone far but that logic doesn't stop a mother reaching full blown panic mode. Which very, very, quickly arrived at my door. I simply couldn't find him anywhere, I was running all over the place shouting:

"Where is James, have you seen my boy? Anyone seen a young boy on his own?" but there was no sighting anywhere by anyone and this was getting serious. As I paused to take stock of the situation, this guy came up to me and said:

"Are you ok, you seem really worried?"

"My God yes I am, I can't find my son he has totally vanished" I replied barely being able to breathe.

"I will help you don't worry."

In a normal situation I would have been bowled over by his cuteness and big cheeky smile, but this was different I was in total meltdown. It didn't matter to me that Harry Styles was now helping me find James, I just wanted to have my son back.

We both ran around everywhere. Harry was opening cupboards, shouting out James name, looking into side rooms, everything. Where the hell was he??

Harry finally suggested the Judge's room as the only place left, but I dismissed that as the security on the door would have been too tight for James to have gone through and it wasn't going to be appropriate for us to just barge our way in anyway.

Harry didn't care, he was after all Harry from One Direction, so he just opened the door and there was Louis Walsh, there was a producer of the show and there was Master James Cundy with the biggest grin I had ever seen playing a board game with both of them.

Harry was quite simply so kind, so caring and I will never forget what he was like that night. I interviewed One Direction many times, after but my favourite will always be my favourite.

Chris Rea

One winters day I had the flu. I pretty much never take to my bed but this day I did, as the woman version of man flu came to me and I lay pathetically under the sheets telling everyone I had Ebola and would no doubt die soon.

The phone kept ringing and I didn't want to answer but it was persistent so probably wasn't the double glazing sales call we all hang up on. It turned out to be a friend of mine who worked at a record company. He said:

"Lizzie honey, where are you right now?"

I coughed back that I was so poorly I expected to be in intensive care shortly, but why was he asking?

"That's such a shame Lizzie as Chris Rea has asked for you especially to feature in his Christmas pop video which is being filmed today."

I suddenly woke up and spluttered out "Chris Rea as in the actual Chris Rea?"

"Yep that's the one Lizzie."

I jumped out of bed, Ebola suddenly cured and said to my friend "20 minutes darling don't worry I'm coming, I will be there!"

I put my lip gloss on and snivelled my way to a film studio just around the corner from me arriving at the allotted 20 minutes I had given myself. It was probably the only time in my life I have ever been on time.

When I got there my world was temporarily shattered.

"Chris Rea won't be here today I'm afraid, didn't we mention that, he isn't in the actual film" said the video team director.

My excitement at meeting him which cured my Ebola was thrown into the bin of despair, and my women flu version of man flu, aka Ebola, immediately returned.

But then I paused. I realised something. Hang on, wow this was proper fame, the fame you have when you are actually too famous to appear in your own video. So, I want to be part of that!

So, I'm in the video for 'Driving Home for Christmas'. The video director did the gentlemanly thing and dressed an ill lady shivering with flu in a short sparkly turquoise dress, and made her dance around a lot in the freezing cold with other celebrities. But the 1988 'Driving Home for Christmas' video, for one of Chris' most iconic songs, is a piece of music history I am very proud to have been a part of, though tinged with some sadness as a dear friend of mine Kristian Digby who starred alongside me and the others in the film, was found dead a few months after filming.

Every Christmas when the video is shown I get to see Kristian's handsome face though and us all having a ball dancing around in the snow. That's a great memory and I'm forever thankful to Chris Rea for that.

Though I never did get to meet him.

Weegate

I stayed at Anthea Turner's house some nights in the summer of 2018 and one morning on Eamonn and Ruth's ITV show I happened to mention that I had weed in her shower, arguing that "When the hot water hits you it's hard not to and it does wash away."

Well, I may have just as well have said that I had an orgy in there as the reaction it caused was way over the top.

Etiquette coach William Hanson on the show with me wasn't believing the two shouldn't mix, twitter started to debate it, and even a survey was instantly done which vindicated me as 72% follow the wee in shower strategy.

In a *you couldn't make it up* moment, the headlines were there online and in the papers and one in particular came out with:

'Anthea Turner bleaches her shower after Lizzie Cundy's toilet trouble.'

My toilet trouble?? The UK was now talking about my 'toilet trouble'?! Friends who I was due to go out with that night called me up concerned saying that as the table for dinner wasn't close to the toilet, I wouldn't embarrass them would I, as they liked that restaurant and went there a lot?

A guy then text me who I had been on a recent date with saying that I should have told him, because it could have gotten a bit frisky that night, and he hadn't been prepared for any issues that may have arisen because of my *trouble*.

Carry on Lizzie at its finest my darlings!

And what can you possibly learn from this? Well, keep your shower stories to yourself I suggest darlings. Just like a trip to Vegas with your friends, what happens in the shower stays in the shower.

Or actually, let's hope it doesn't!

Meghan Markle

It was late 2013 and I was booked to do the red carpet TV interviews for a charity event hosted by Eva Longoria. The night before that though, there was a private dinner which I had been invited to at the house of John Caudwell, the mobile phone billionaire.

They sat me next to a lady named Meghan Markle. She had been starring in Suits, a hit show in the USA, that at the time not many of us in the UK had heard about. Meghan and I naturally didn't have a clue who either of us were. That has never stopped me before though and it was very quickly clear it hadn't ever stopped her either.

"Oh, babes how are you, so nice to meet you" she opened up with hugging me and that started an evening of drinking, dancing and non-stop laughing between us.

It was very obvious that she loved being in London and very quickly wanted to know where the best members clubs and restaurants were. As they would compete to be my expert subjects on Mastermind, we gelled like the hair of an 80's pop star, so much so that I couldn't recall the next day who was actually sat on the other side of me. We did selfies together we mucked around together and I remember her being so impressed that she was meeting the Beckham's the very next night. I didn't have the heart to tell her she was heading for disappointment if she was expecting a crazy wild night out with Victoria.

Then the obvious thing that was going to happen, happened. We started chatting about guys.

"I just love London babes, but where are those British guys? How do I meet them?" she interrogated me, probably on the very correct assumption I would naturally know the answer, before adding for absolute clarity "actually babes, do you know any nice famous men?"

So, I did the polite thing which was to get out my mobile phone, flick through the contacts and hand her Prince Harry's Number. The rest my darlings is what they call history.

Ok, ok, I may not have done that but you believed it for second didn't you?

The next night I ran into her again on the red carpet at the charity event, when I did an interview for OK! TV. This was despite my cameraman's reluctance who said we should ignore her as no one would know who she was.

Not then maybe, but they sure do now.

"Hi babes, I just love London, though not the weather" she said and we carried on as we did the previous night when the interview was over. She figured, I guess, that I was a better bet for that than Victoria would be.

We kept in touch and I text her to say *"Great catch"* when I heard the news about Harry some 2 years later.

Kim Kardashian

I was on the red carpet at the Fifi UK fragrance awards in 2012 which was an event featuring Kim Kardashian's new perfume. The great lady herself was going to attend.

"We want some front page news!" said Richard Desmond my terrifying friend, and I went to the event feeling very determined but also cheeky, especially when the very nervous PR lady there lectured us all at the start about only having 2 questions each for Kim and not one of them should be about her bottom! Yep, we had a bum warning. One question had to be about perfume too as well. So, talking about her boobs was ok then but not her bottom.

"Don't mention the war, don't mention the war" it did just seem like a Fawlty Towers sketch.

Showbiz of course immediately said we had to mention the *war*, aka bottom, which is exactly what I was thinking we had to do too, so the naughty bum gang waited for the call and then it came.

"Ok your turn now."

But before we got to see Kim, we got the final bum warning from Basil Fawlty in PR as we made our way through the ever growing entourage that accompanies her. It was more intense than some royal events I've been to with the security detail there as well. Kim liked me immediately I could tell, well the fact she held my hand straight away probably helped me form that conclusion, and we talked about perfume, London, the usual things as the PR and security military faction got ever closer to the rebels Cundy and Showbiz, aka Butch Cassidy and the Sundance Kid.

I went for it, it was now or never Cunders Kid!

"I've got to ask you Kim, just how did you get that wonderful bum?" I enquired.

And she laughed her head off, and talked about her bottom whilst the PR's face went paler and paler and the desire to throw us out got larger and larger. But then KK asked me to join her inside and sat her next to me through the whole event.

Oh, well why not!

And for an hour we became new best mates, with everyone thinking, not for the first time, "How did you get invited in?" but it was just one of those nights where everything went to plan. She was just a lovely sweet lady and we had a few drinks and laughed a lot, swapping numbers and we still stay in touch, even now.

From my red carpet escapades, it has to be said I had started to compile an award-winning mobile phone contacts list. But I had also picked up numbers from some people that I really didn't want to see again. I used to put those names into my phone with entries like 'Don't want to talk to you' or 'strange guy, don't answer' and one such man I put in as 'most boring man ever'.

I happened to be out at a party one day and he was there. I lost my phone and went into panic.

"Hey don't worry" he said, "I will ring it for you from my phone."

As it started to ring, it was clearly on the table right next to him and I suddenly realised what name would flash up if he got his hands on it. I hurled myself across the room just as he was headed for it and got to it first by some miracle.

"My God you love that phone" he said which was in fact the most interesting thing he ever did say to me.

Sharon Stone

I was in Butler and Wilson the jewellery shop in Fulham, the day before a big Ball I was arranging for a cancer charity, and I was after this big choker they had on display, very thick but would work well with the outfit I was going to wear. It was vintage but cool, and I paraded in front of the mirror before eventually taking it off whilst I carried on looking around for a while as women often do despite the fact they already know they wanted the first thing they tried on.

As I'm browsing, in walks Sharon Stone, who I had never met before, with her sister and she immediately sees the choker and tries it on.

"You do look great in that" I said to her "I was going to get it."

We got chatting about the event I was hosting and I cheekily asked if they would come along later which she said she would think about, lovely to meet you etc.

Then, as she is walking out, I get a tap on the shoulder and as I turned around Sharon said to me "I can't make it, but here is the choker I bought it for you, I wanted you to have it and to look gorgeous in it."

You couldn't make it up. What a lady! We exchanged numbers and have remained close friends ever since.

Tom Cruise

As part of my red carpet series, I interviewed Tom Cruise for the film he was starring in, The Edge of Tomorrow, and managed to grab him for a one-to-one, which often is much harder than you imagine it would be. You have a split second to get on well with someone or they will get distracted by the constant shouting of "Over here!" by another presenter. In this case, it worked with Tom instantly, we got a good piece on film and in we all went to the movie theatre for the premiere. Only for most us to then walk straight out of the movie theatre, via the back door when the coast was clear to go off to do other things. Which I duly did as most do too at a premiere. They have already seen it they don't have to relive it.

I met my son Josh outside and we jumped into a quick cab to take us to Cecconi's on the corner of Saville Row for something to eat before we headed home. As we got into the restaurant, Josh started to hit me on the arm saying "Mum, mum someone is waving at you" which I hadn't seen and I dismissed him away as I was getting a table which is far from easy to arrange there.

Josh was, however, persistent:

"Mum, mum" he tried again.

"Shhhhhh Josh" I replied again.

"Mum, mum."

Basically, repeat times 5 and you get the picture until he finally, finally, gets to the point:

"But mum there is a man who looks a lot like Tom Cruise over there calling you over to his table."

"See you Josh!" I said abandoning my son in a millisecond, but remembering to shout out over my shoulder to him full of maternal concern:

"But guard our table!"

I went right over and plonked myself next to the man who looked a lot like Tom Cruise, because he was Tom Cruise. He was there with the director of the film and recognised me from the red carpet meeting we had just had.

"Come here Lizzie, sit down and hang out for a bit" he said smiling and my God did that man have nice teeth.

So, I sat down and to my utter shame readers I sat there for a good 20 minutes, whilst my son Josh guarded the table trying to get my attention all the time as Tom was one of his big heroes. But Tom and I we were just laughing and laughing, and it's hard when you laugh with Tom Cruise to not get carried away by a laughing Tom Cruise. He was cheeky, had a wonderful energy

When the realisation slowly hit me that I may have been a tad selfish abandoning my son, whilst hogging the limelight, I said goodbye to TC (obviously best mates by then so I can use initials now) and went back to my table, sitting down casually as if I had just been to the loo.

"Have you ordered for me darling?" I asked Josh as he went into total meltdown over his mother's actions and steak and chips for him was not going to make up for it apparently. He eventually got a wave from TC (still best mates) as he left, which I thought would make up for it, but apparently didn't compare to me sitting and laughing with him for 20 minutes.

I can't imagine why?!

<u>Bond Girl</u>

I became a Bond girl. Well, of sorts. More like a Bond leg girl.

Pierce Brosnan was starring in Goldeneye in 1994 and I got a call from the studio to say that they needed a body double for Izabella Scorupco who played the female lead for the film. I had only just given birth to Josh and was breastfeeding, but they said that wasn't a problem, it was my legs they were mainly after, so off I trotted to the glamorous Watford where part of the film was being shot on an airfield nearby.

They let me bring Josh along for some days, and I was desperate to get working again so it seemed the perfect job for that very moment.

I got on instantly with Pierce. What a lovely man, great Irish fun and he had the biggest trailer on the set, naturally. He told me one day, rather foolishly, I could use it if I wanted to as there was so much hanging around. So off I went with a friend who was with me that day and inside, wow! There was so much artwork in there, he was a fantastic painter. But I felt mischievous and so to prove that motherhood had indeed matured me. I started to show off in the Bondmobile trying on his clothes, larking around for a change and then I happened to see his toothbrush in the corner. Naturally, I have to then brush mine with it and in-between gargling I was shouting out to my friend that I am using James Bond's toothbrush because that is a very cool thing to do, don't you know!

Not, therefore the right moment for Pierce Brosnan, 007, to walk in which he indeed did!

"Elizabeth, what exactly are you doing with my toothbrush?" was his Bond-like observation to me, and I could find no sensible reply to that other than "is there any floss about Pierce?"

He took it all in his stride and then just took the mickey out of me for the rest of the location shoot. He was one of the nicest guys I have ever met, and we just giggled and giggled, which didn't help the camera crew though on some shots when we were supposed to be doing a love scene. I then did a further two Bond films as a body double before my body, well started to double itself with motherhood and age, and my Bond career was over without anyone really knowing I ever had a Bond career.

But I am a 3 time Bond girl and that must be close to some sort of world record.

Johnny Depp

Sometimes you just can't get hold of the star on the red carpet. The main TV channels go first in line, then newspapers, then *others*. And we were part of the *others* which is just above the popcorn sellers in the pecking order. So, every filming we ever did on a red carpet was a bun fight at the O.K. Corral, which was in fact ironically appropriate as were filming mostly for OK!

When Johnny Depp came over to promote the Lone Ranger which was to put it mildly, a stinker of a film, we just couldn't get near him, so faced with no footage Showbiz and I stood there pondering and our eyes at the same time moved towards some poo on the red carpet that one of the 'Lone Ranger's' horses had left.

We walked over to it and I said to tape "Here is my review of the film and what's it like" and Showbiz panned down to the pile of poo at my feet. That's improvising at its very best right there my darlings, and was factually accurate at the same time, the point being made through the use of shit imagery. Literally. I still think we should have won an award for that clip!

Sometimes you get the names confused on a red carpet though even if you know the stars as the pressure starts to mount on you.

At an award show once, I kept shouting "Brian, Brian over here" to Graham Norton so he would come over. Now I know Graham and I don't know who Brian is, but I still kept shouting "Brian" none the less and got very upset later at how rude Graham had been to me, until Showbiz pointed out he probably didn't know who Brian was either.

The Cannes Film festival

I was at the Cannes film festival in 2012 as a guest of Eva Longoria who was hosting a massive charity gala dinner there. On the guest list were multiple A-list celebrities including Jane Fonda and Mariah Carey, and I was just taking it all in when Eva came rushing over to me, a few hours before it started, and pleaded desperately:

"Darling what are you doing tonight?"

Before I could answer that with the bleeding obvious e.g. I'm at your dinner Eva, she carried on with...

"Because you are now co-hosting the event, you simply have to someone has pulled out and I need you."

And that was that. No time to discuss my rider, the size of my trailer, my make-up, the type of flowers I wanted, the bags of cashew nuts I required. Nothing. But I was excited none the less to be asked.

My co-host was a famous Russian TV presenter, described to me at the time as the Philip Schofield of Moscow, which I assumed did not mean he once starred on TV with Gordon the Gopher. The trouble was his English was as good as my Russian which meant it was rubbish basically as I only knew the words 'Ra Ra Rasputin'. That apparently didn't make me fluent.

No rehearsal, straight in we went, and Mr Moscow goes out first to the audience of A-listers. I am backstage now, not at all nervous, simply ready for the moment where just like at the Oscars, the male presenter will no doubt begin with saying many wonderful things about his lady co-host. Then the music will start and gliding onto the stage, indeed dare I say waltzing, will come Princess Elizabeth of Richmond. The stage would be her majestic kingdom, her media destiny finally fulfilled, and she would shine like a pure diamond in the clear Mediterranean night sky.

But, instead, my presenting partner welcomed me out with the immortal words:

"Pleaze be welcumming to join on stage me for zis night, ma go-hosty... Linzsay Cunty!"

No music as I came on, no fanfare, just the sound of my friends in the audience whooping and laughing at my walk of shame towards the microphone. I tried to reason with Rasputin:

"My name is Cundy."

"I noze, yew arse a Cunty" he replied.

"No... Cundy" I said in exasperation.

"Yeeez, zits what I zed, you ave lovely Cunty." he exclaimed all pleased with his new found mastery of the English language.

In the end, I just shut up and agreed.

In fairness, he may have been right anyway. Especially with the 'lovely' bit.

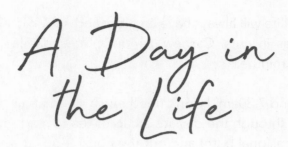

A Day in the Life

"Her best qualities? For me it's her ability to integrate with anyone and work a room. To this day I've never seen anything like it. She somehow manages to always remain charming and create a conversation with anyone she comes across. For me that's her best quality. I wish I could talk the way she does. Mum also has a ridiculous sense of humour, the same silly dances at random moments, weird voices and she's very, very quick witted.

I have honestly never Googled my mum, so I wouldn't know about what pictures may appear online about her. I know they're there, but it has never bothered me. She looks how she looks and some people want to look like that, and others don't. She can do what she likes as far as I'm concerned.

I thought she was great on Shirley Valentine. It was a brilliantly made show though, which helped. But she came across as she really is - which is what I wanted to happen the most. Because I know who she is and others don't, they make judgements. For her to be, and come across as, herself was the best possible result because she's too amazing to not shine.

But I don't think she has changed after the show was filmed. Not particularly. It's very difficult to change the core of a person after just one month. But I will admit she's learnt a few Greek dishes which are very nice, and the new hairstyle really suits her.

My friends think she is really cool. My really close friends get to meet her of course and she's very charming to all of them. I recently brought a girlfriend around for the first time and they got on really well, which was always going to be the case with mum anyway.

She's kind, funny, charming, incredibly likeable, loves a drink and a joke. But she can be incredibly frustrating at times, she's usually always late and a nightmare with parking fines.

But she can get away with murder if she wanted to with me."

Josh Cundy – Lizzie's oldest son

My daily life will always have lip gloss and nuts in it. No, not them. Nuts as in nuts. Cashew, almonds, macadamia - I could eat them every minute.

I wake around 7.30am, I don't need much sleep at all, 5 or so hours will get me through the day. It's a cup of tea to start, milk no sugar, shower (occasional bath) and out the house I go, at that stage with just a little make-up on and of course the lip gloss. Always the lip gloss, no matter what. Sunshine or rain it goes on and I could apply it in my sleep, I'm that practised. I may have to ferry James about somewhere who still lives at home and then on the way back I will go to the gym for a 40 minute workout which I like to do on average 4 times a week. Arm weights, crunches, no running but a bit of bike work to end the session.

When I get back home it's more often than not a quick turnaround to get ready for an event in London. I'm rarely at home all day and night on any day. I live out of London though in Hampshire, and it's an hour or so into town from there so there is a fair bit of driving involved in Cundy's daily routine. I may take an extra dress with me for later but I will drive into town wearing what I'm going to wear to the event. I can park up at various little hotspots in London I've arranged over the years.

If it's an event with lunch then I will usually always pour water into any alcohol given to me. If it's not an event, I usually have a salad. I may hang out in one of London's members clubs in the afternoon if I'm also doing anything in the evening but will try and get home no later than 11pm if I do. Sometimes event organisers will send cars for me but most of the time I just drive there and back.

When I get in, no matter how late, I will unwind at home, have a cup of tea, catch up on anything I've missed on TV and especially the main celebrity programmes which I need to keep up to date on for my shows on FUBAR and Talk Radio.

My radio career started over 3 years ago, when I was asked to go on as a guest with co-host Mark Dowlen. The next day I had a call from the Furbar boss Duncan Smith and was offered to co-host the show, taking over from Katie Price who had previously been doing it. I was on a radio roll as they then asked me to do the whole thing on my own making it much more showbiz orientated. That has now moved on to me presenting on Thursday, Friday and Saturday early evenings with Stephen Leng. I just love it. It has a cult following and a young vibrant audience.

Guests know the show is like a party and anything goes. Which it often does, including marriage proposals (which I was so shocked about I fell off my chair) and the footballer Jermaine Pennant telling us about 3 threesomes he had with Ashley Cole.

I have only missed 3 shows in 3 years. I believe strongly in hard work and I do not recall ever missing an event I was booked for either.

Sometimes when I get in late I like to watch the politics shows like Question Time. I got into politics through my father's connections with the Conservative Party and I know people like Nigel Farage and David Davies. Nigel showed up once unexpectedly at a party I was at and it was like the parting of the Red Sea as he made his way through the venue. I've known him for ages, way before Brexit but he can be a bit of a devil, which is why I suppose the public warm to him. He is also bloody clever, though not as clever as the cleverest person alive.

And who is that?

Well, Stephen Fry of course!

And he is also the most charming man alive too.

I first met Stephen at a charity stroke event and we got talking. It turned out my mother is friends with his mother and they all socialise in Norfolk together. He has been so helpful to Josh in his acting and he is simply a lovely kind Einstein of a man.

On a Sunday I just like to be lazy. But I never wear casual clothes, I'm always glam. I was a *grid girl* once and when they banned it recently I said I strongly disagreed with that. My argument was that those girls have been stopped from making a living. I had the time of my life when I did it, which is another one of the reasons I stood up for those girls, because I know from my own experience that they are so well looked after. I love Formula One. I met all of the racing drivers when I was a grid girl and they all treated us with total respect. It was one of the best times ever, so I did find it really sad that the PC Brigade came in and said there cannot be anything like that anymore saying 'it's degrading' ignoring the fact it actually made a good living for them and they were very happy doing it.

On a Sunday if I can go to watch a Chelsea game with my boys then that would be perfect, but I will always go to the gym regardless and get the papers on the way home. I love to make a roast and, in the evening, go for a drink in the local village pub which has a nice cosy fire. I simply love Sundays and both my boys are normally with me then.

My boys in the daily life of Cunders?

Well Josh is now 24 and James 18. They are in my 'gang' and are still very much part of everything in my world.

Josh is an actor now and is at drama school. He is the more sensible one of my two boys, safely sensible and he will be the chief instigator of rebellion against anything I may want to wear out that is too racy. I always wanted boys not girls and so I'm blessed to have them. Josh was an easy birth, no problems before or after and I took to motherhood immediately. I had no real bump until I was 6 months in and gave birth with no drugs as I like my mind to always be in control. For the record, my waters broke after a hot curry so old wives tale or not, it worked for me!

I loved being a mum but wanted Josh with me all the time on any work I was doing and even got him some modelling jobs as a baby, which led to him being in adverts from an early age. He has then also done some modelling and TV work.

Josh is a cool dude. One laid back cool dude.

A couple of years ago, he and I were on our way back in the car from some event, driving through Richmond, when we got stuck in a bit of traffic. I stopped the car but then somehow lurched forward a little, by mistake, and hit the back of the motor in front of me. It only seemed to be a gentle bump so I didn't immediately get out to look, hoping it was a non-event and the driver of the other car hadn't noticed it.

Well he had noticed.

Out of that car came this huge guy, absolutely massive, very scary looking and he didn't look happy. At all. I made the instant decision that this needed to be dealt with and confronted head on, so pushed Josh out of the car to do exactly that for me, locking the car doors behind me. It was part of life's training for him darlings in case you think I was being a scaredy cat chicken shit, who wasn't taking responsibility for their own mistakes.

As I sat safely in the front seat of my car, the guy outside, who Josh is having his life coach training session with, is getting really mad and starts to point in a frantic pointy way to something in the back of his car. Josh, being the cool dude he is, just shrugged his shoulders as if to say "There doesn't look anything wrong to me there mate" and started to take some pictures of the *damage* in a foolish act of bravery, when the man mountains next move is probably to bear hug you, throw you to the floor and jump up and down on your crown jewels until your voice is set to be high pitched forever more. I then wound the window down very bravely, I thought about a quarter of an inch, to offer motherly concern and solidarity to Josh but heard Mr Mountain, whose English wasn't that great, demanding that Josh handed over 'his papers' which then resulted in both of them staring and pointing at me.

"What's it got to with me?" I thought and then remembered "oh yeah everything" as I gestured to Josh to come back inside the car mouthing that I would get the 'papers' for him. Josh mouthed back there was nothing wrong with this guy's car at all but came back none-the-less.

I may then just have escalated the tiny dramarama just a little bit too much readers by shouting to Josh "Lets go!" as soon as he had sat back inside the car, at the very same time as sticking my foot down on the accelerator in order to make our dramatic escape from tyranny.

Mr Mountain selfishly wasn't giving up on his quest for 'the papers' though. He jumped onto the bonnet of my car like he was the stunt man on a Bond movie and hanged on for dear life, half on half off, as I did the correct thing in these situations, which wasn't to break and maturely discuss the issues at hand, but instead to carry on driving and put the window wipers on to try and push an 18 stone 6ft 6 giant off of my car. Then, almost in slow motion, he just slowly slides off the bonnet like it was a piece of butter in a pan and ended up face down on the pavement.

Thinking that was the end of that as we drive off, immediately a small traffic jam appeared in front of us which was the worst kind of sods law. Mountain man takes that opportunity to jump into his car, and as we sped away from the traffic there he was behind us gesturing in his front windscreen a not appropriate gesture to show a lady I have to say. So then began a chase around Richmond like it was a scene from Smokey and the Bandit, me driving down side road after side road trying to shake him before my local knowledge finally won the day in the mad mad chase and we finally lost him.

The Richmond Grand Prix victory was mine!

It took a good couple of minutes to get my breath back and start driving again. We hadn't said say a single word to each during the chase and after. The silence was broken by the laid back cool dude Josh, "So, what's for dinner tonight then mum?" as we turned onto the A3 and headed home for fish and chips. Again.

James, my youngest son, was in some ways a miracle baby. When Jason's cancer was first detected we were warned that surgery and radiotherapy would likely leave him infertile. We took a sperm sample very early in the cancer treatment in case that actually did happen and we could then try for IVF if we wanted to.

But in the end we didn't need it and against every single set of odds, I became pregnant.

James arrived early. He just wanted to get out of my tummy and get on with his life. He showed that by always wriggling anyway as the months of pregnancy wore on and from the very moment of me giving birth he has been 100 miles an hour, with an energy my God I wish I had. Now, James is keen on a football career and in-between trials he works at Talk Sport.

I will ring my boys at least 3 times a day if I'm not with them and my mum once a day.

I do get recognised on a daily basis when I do the basic things like supermarket shopping, but pretty much no matter what the circumstances are, I will stop and talk with people, sign anything and do selfies. The selfie thing in particular I think you owe people, as it is they who have put you where you are.

But regardless of that, I also frankly just like meeting people which is why I will chat longer than you would imagine a 'celebrity' ever would do.

Unlike I have to say Bruce Willis who hates selfies and it seems hates meeting people.

I was doing my ITV at the Movies show and we were in Leicester Square for the premiere of a movie that he was in. As I looked down the red carpet waiting for him to pass where I was, he generally didn't seem to be bonding with anyone and most importantly not with the fans either. He was the rudest celebrity I have ever met, though I may have gotten things off to a bad start by shouting "Brucie, Brucie can I have a word?" as he grumpily walked past me.

He looked at me, snapped his fingers angrily and said "My name is not Brucie." Which was a bugger as my next line was going to be "Higher than a 3 you say?"

He then proceeded to answer every one of my questions to him with the question itself.

Like this:

"Tell me Bruce (ie) what did you like best about the film?" says Lizzie which let's face it, wasn't a Jeremy Paxman opening, and so he should therefore have warmed to it.

"I don't know, you tell me what you liked best" he came back to me with thinking it was such a funny reply.

"What did you think of the casting?" I asked not laughing at all at his previous attempt at a joke.

"I think we should hear you tell me what you thought of the acting?" was his response.

Etc. etc.

What a complete knob!

It was like interviewing myself and all the time he just stared at me without blinking. He was a very strange man. I wasn't backing down and it developed into a frosty minute. All I could see was Showbiz Simon in the background, shoulders shaking in laughter as the Brucie battle of the red carpet continued. I thought 'you aren't intimidating me mate' and didn't back down at any point in the chat.

Food is very important in my life. I have had eating disorders at various times in my teenage years and those are the sort of things that never leave you, well never leave your mind anyway. The first time it happened to me, my mum thought she would lose me, it had gotten that bad.

Still to this day it upsets me greatly remembering what I put my family through and especially my mum. I was 14 and increasingly becoming unhappy with the nun's treatment of me at school. I just wanted to go to drama school and do my modelling. I felt I was different to the others in class and therefore should be allowed to do different things. Mum and Dad were not getting on particularly well at that time, and as I couldn't control my schooling, I could control my food and so that is what I did with my unhappiness.

Basically, I gave up eating and started to become anorexic.

Covering up your eating is easy until of course your weight loss becomes obvious. The act of hiding or throwing your food away became easy to me. The nuns and mum were not stupid though and as the months wore on they became increasingly more and more concerned.

It took a boy to snap me out of the spiral downwards into total oblivion. Martin Leicester Grey, a boy who I really fancied came up to me one day and said "You would be so lovely if you weren't so thin" and that was that. I would have walked over hot coals for that boy so I started to eat normally once more and eventually ended up seeing him. I was under 5 stone at that point though and my cheek bones were even starting to show. I had had a year of an eating disorder.

It has resurfaced a few more times over my life, when I was nearly raped and when my marriage was heading for real difficulties. You never really lose it, it is inside you waiting to reappear at a vulnerable moment.

Sometimes events I do are for my charitable work which has been important to me for the last 20 years. I started my work when Jason got the news about his testicular cancer and over the years I've come to the firm conclusion that celebrities do make a massive difference.

Some though, try and charge for attending a charity event which is astonishing I have to say, and even worse let down the organisers at the last minute. I would never charge a charity for anything and over the years have not only attended many functions, but organised them too as I can bring in 'names' which will help promote the charity's aims. This in turn leads to better fundraising for them.

I have an interest with Simon Cowell in the dog's charity in Barbados, where animals it has to be said are not treated well and I was instrumental in 'Lucy's Law' which helped stop puppy farming in the UK. Simon does things in particular that no one would ever hear about, and he doesn't do it for any publicity, he does it for kindness.

I will go to church at least twice a week and just sit there with my thoughts and I always light a candle for someone. When I walk away from church I always feel stronger, always feel a better person. My faith is very important to me and has been all my life. It has gotten me through the dark times and I have always been religious, getting it from my mum who is very Christian and spiritual in general. I believe in the afterlife and I believe those that you have loved in this life you will meet again to love even after you die. I strongly think there is a reason why we are all here. I will say a little prayer when I wake up and when I go to bed I will always say a prayer of thanks. I'm not fanatical in the born again Christian evangelical way but none-the-less my faith is important to me and it is calming for me.

It was so important when I married that it was a proper catholic wedding, in a church with a catholic service. Jason wasn't catholic which would obviously be a problem in that grand plan, but I didn't give up and I eventually concluded that priests love wine and football, so I invited the one I wanted around to my place at Chelsea Harbour and started the red wine session. We got chatting about football and fitness in general, which then led to me showing him how to do squats. Just at that moment Jason walks in to see his future bride and a priest going up and down in the front room, but it worked, sealed with the promise of a few more bottles of red wine.

In the autumn of 2011 I thought I would try something completely different to make sense of my life and what had happened to me. It was called past life transgression which was basically a process where you are hypnotised to sleep to find out if your past life could explain your current life. It was to be featured in a new Channel 4 show and I was under the instruction of specialist Nicolas Aujula, who was frankly weird and had more make-up on than me.

As I was put into a deep sleep, something really bizarre started to happen. I apparently started to reveal the life of Anne Boleyn, the 2nd wife of King Henry VIII. I described in detail her desperation as she had to contend with the fiery temper of the King, and it became clear that I was describing myself as Anne, so that in a past life I was actually her.

I talked about both Hampton Court and The Tower of London in a way I could never possibly have known, and I went over the panic of knowing that I was about to be beheaded And my reaction when I woke? I wasn't surprised. I was I suppose at the detail, but not by the concept.

Now I know that you are thinking, what a load of old nonsense she is going on about, but honestly, I knew nothing about Anne Boleyn. I may have studied her at school as a teenager for a brief moment, but certainly not since, and couldn't recall what I had learnt at school now anyway, when of course I had actually bothered to turn up.

Nicolas though did not help the believability by completely hamming it up with this summary "It is clear that Lizzie has brought back the old relationship dynamics regarding self worth and power. By letting go of these I feel she has now rediscovered her own voice and ability to be assertive."

I am very spiritual though. I believe in the stars and horoscopes and use them to see if I will get on with someone in advance of meeting. I think I may be a little bit psychic as well. There were distinct similarities between Anne and I in the dominating of us by our men, and so I don't dismiss the possibilities of who I may have been in a previous life.

My God I can just imagine the headlines the press will have now commenting on this part of the book:

'Cundy says she is the real Queen, Elizabeth III, and plans to gets her knockers out at the Coronation.'

'Henry cut Cundy's head off to shut her up once, can't he do it again?'

'Cundy makes a great case why Britain should now be a republic.'

I can only see one advantage to me though if I was actually the Queen.

It would be far easier for me to blag my way into something.

"Are you on the guest list love?"

"No, I am the bloody Queen young man so sod off and let me in."

The Summer That Saved Me

"Mum has loads of really great qualities. She is so laid back (probably too laid-back) she's very funny and extremely generous. But she is incredibly messy at home!!

I loved watching her on Shirley Valentine because she was very much herself and opened up more about her past, having similar types of women around her to feed off, which I think did her the world of good.

My friends think she is funny. She always burns pizzas when they come over so I always get stick for her cooking but they like her because she is laid-back. If I wanted to have a party of about 50 people on Saturday she would definitely be cool with it.

She has a weird addiction to peanuts and biscuits when she's at home so whenever I go into the front room, there are always biscuit crumbs or a few peanuts lying on the table.

I always find it amazing how she could somehow charm a restaurant owner into getting us a table even though the place is fully booked!

When I was younger at school, if I was feeling tired on a particular day and wanted the morning off school, she would always cover for me, phone the school to say I was coming in late or even just let me have the day off itself. That always makes me smile even to this day.

I am the luckiest son ever born to have such a lovely mum. She would always drive endless hours to drop me off for football training, she would always get me my favourite toys, she would always make me the food I wanted, she would always make me laugh, always let me watch sport and always let me stay up late on a school night!

My brother and I are very, very blessed to have her."

James Cundy – Lizzie's youngest son

As the beginning of 2018 started I just felt flat. Ok, most of us start that way at the beginning of a year, but this was different it had been building up for a while. It was difficult to pinpoint exactly why, I had a good year in 2017, lots of work and home life was excellent. But then it hit me.

I was feeling drained by people.

Suddenly meeting them at all these events started to get to me. I know this sounds mean, but I was feeling like as soon as I went to any party or promotion event, the moment I stepped in I just wanted to leave. I couldn't wait to get home. I could feel I was unhappy and I remember some nights driving home with tears running down my face. I felt a sadness and emptiness I hadn't experienced before even within the dark days of my marriage break-up. I was becoming drained by other's energy when normally I would just feed of it. One day I went to the theatre and just went home at the interval. I was becoming fed up with 'wear this, wear that' routine, I just wanted to wear what I wanted to and be who I wanted to be.

I felt I had been on the run since 2010 and was it Lizzie Miller or Lizzie Cundy I wanted to be for the rest of my life?

It was becoming clear that instead of being subservient to a husband I was being subservient now to a lifestyle in its place. I simply wasn't enjoying 'brand Lizzie' anymore, and I wanted to stop the wheel and get off.

To be more precise, stop the celebrity wheel, I want to get off!

Now I know many would love to be on that wheel and reading this will think, my God you try having my job, and I understand totally that point but we all react in different ways and unhappiness is unhappiness. I'm just being honest about myself at that very moment in my life.

For so long, bad reviews or comments about me went flying over my head. I just didn't care about them, but now I was thinking that half the people I meet don't like me and have no real good intentions towards me so why should I keep putting myself through that treadmill? The TV work I still very much enjoyed, but it was the nights out that I didn't. But both brought me the income I still needed. I was starting to see the whole industry in a different light and I was falling lower and lower into borderline depression the more I thought about it.

Then, a lifeline appeared in the form of a bubbly energetic gorgeous blonde lady. Her name was Vickie White of White Management one of the top showbiz managers in the country and who was my agent too.

She called me up in early February.

"There is a show you may be interested in babes it's about middle-aged women who want to make a new life for themselves and it is set in Greece."

It took me one second to reply.

"My God, right now a break away from the UK is exactly what I need and I know Greece well, we used to holiday each year there when I was younger. I love the idea!"

As the chat continued, we both agreed that for people to start taking me more seriously I needed to break away and do a show like this. But for me this wasn't just about a career, it was about my total sanity which was starting to slip away from me as the days of 2018 started to click on by.

I had to have this show, it had to be mine. It was to be called Shirley Valentine's Summer and would feature 8 well known ladies spending a month together in pursuit of love and self-discovery. After weeks of back and forth with Vickie and the show's producers they didn't seem that keen on the idea of Lizzie Cundy but Vickie, being the magnificent manager that she is, kept at it to try and get me a chance. There is always a way in life and finally in this case there was. They agreed to have a chat and I was asked to come in as soon as I could for a meeting.

The morning of the casting I went into my local church, lit a candle and prayed. But this time I prayed for myself and not for others as I had done hundreds of times over the years before. For the first time ever, it was about me. I needed to love myself again.

The casting went really well. The producer Stef Aleksander, such a lovely lady, was one of those people that you want as your friend and you warm too instantly. We laughed so much, even if she had said I wasn't any good for the role I would still have liked to hang out with her afterwards. But what she did say in particular and what so many say to me, was that this 'Lizzie' was not what she had excepted at all. *Real Lizzie* is not like *caricature Lizzie*. I have to confess now though it was helped that day by me toning it right down for our meeting, wearing a very conservative polo neck black dress. The boss, aka my manager Vickie, had given me the very strict instructions earlier in the day that under no circumstances should any tits or legs be shown. Which obviously worked as the titless, legless Cunders got a recall soon after the casting.

The night before it was just so tense. I would imagine you thinking it must be fairly straightforward to get onto a show like that but believe me darlings it isn't. I was up against many names you would recognise and some were my friends.

And after the recall it got even more tense. I received a call from Vickie saying "Babes I don't think this has gone your way, I'm hearing on the grapevine others have been booked" but we persevered and with a last throw of the dice, Vickie sent all of the press I had received the previous year to the show's production team, to remind them of the PR they would be likely to get, which was frankly astonishing when it was all added together.

It was a masterstroke by the master manager!

The phone call I needed for my sanity finally arrived from Blondie the wonder agent.

"Are you sitting down Lizzie because you have got it, you're in babes!"

And that was that. The beginning of the end of my downward spiral.

We were due to leave for Greece in early May. The day before the departure I got a call from the show's production who told me the names of the other ladies who would be on the show with me. When they mentioned one name in particular my heart truly sank as this woman did not like me at all and the feeling in fairness was probably mutual. Though in true school playground fashion, she started it first.

The ladies name was Nancy Dell'Olio.

Nancy Dell'Olio, herein nicknamed Nando, because it is probably just a tad better than Nanny D, and because I will get the spelling wrong at least five times if I use her full name hereafter. Plus, it's juvenile and I'm feeling playful today as I write this. Nando, who you would have read briefly about in the WAGs chapter previously, was the girlfriend of Sven-Göran Eriksson the manager of the England football team at the time of the 2006 World Cup, the moment when WAGmania started.

She had told numerous friends of mine over the years following something along the lines of:

"I was seeing the manager, she was seeing a second rate player, why should I ever talk to her" and for some reason she just didn't like me. Which is presumably then one of the reasons why ITV booked us both to appear together. I knew she would be incredibly hard work to live with, and this was going to be tough, but the boys were so excited for me to go on the show it spurred me on to do the last minute packing of the clothes and shoes I would never wear, and then on to the airport itself I finally went.

This was my chance to be myself and to show everyone what that really meant.

I met one of the show's co-stars, Ingrid Tarrant, at the airport as the production company had decided it was best we didn't all travel together to keep the sense of drama real when we all did meet on camera in Greece itself. We immediately clicked, immediately got on like the clichéd 'house on fire'. Ingrid just talks and talks she doesn't even come up for air, she just keeps going, breathing is secondary to the main task at hand. Talking. She doesn't just talk for England, she talks for Scotland, Wales, Northern Island, the Commonwealth and the British Empire as it stood in all its glory in 1854 too. But she is adorable. Even when she is talking.

This young guy (kid) from the production company had turned up to greet us as we arrived in the departure lounge, and he started to immediately outline the 'rules'. Emmmm, rules don't really work with me and certainly didn't with Ingrid. He had been given the highly stressful job of chaperoning us to Greece which was the poisoned chalice of all chalices.

You can just imagine the scene in the production company offices as the selection for that task was made. Ten people are in a room, someone opens the door suddenly and shouts:

"Quick get out, the production manager is coming and is looking for a volunteer to chaperone Tarrant and Cundy to Greece!" and a mass stampede to get the hell out of the room starts with men and women squeezing through the door to make their escape. And just poor Billy the Kid remained, principally because they had just tied him to a chair.

He did try to keep order though, bless his lovely heart.

"Now, I don't really want you two talking, we want it saved for the show. Please keep with me at all times so I can watch over you and make sure you are keeping to the schedule and itinerary which I will hand out to you in due course when the itinerary says that I can."

As soon as Billy's back was turned Ingrid went shopping. When he turned around and realised he had lost one half of the double act (all be it the noisy half) he went pale. No white. A whiter shade of pale in fact. Her going missing was not on the itinerary apparently and definitely was not in the 'rules'.

"Don't worry, she is a grown woman I'm sure it will all be ok" I reassured him in a reassuring motherly way.

"It won't, it won't, my God what do I do?" he wailed running around in a circle on the spot until he realised it would be better to shout that as he ran around the departure lounge instead looking for the missing Ingrid. I thought the easy way to find her would be to just follow her voice, but he had gone by the time I could helpfully have suggested that.

When he eventually returned with the very naughty Ingrid, I had left to go shopping myself, so the same Billy the Kid routine then followed, though he wisely took The Tarrant with him this time to find me.

"Can you please just stay together, please, please" pleaded Billy the Kid when I was eventually discovered.

We just nodded wisely at him and carried on talking.

"Please don't tell them that you got lost and separated, please."

We just nodded wisely at him and carried on talking.

But this was only the start of his problems, it was just the warm up act by the middle aged cheeky girls before the main event started. The plane journey. The poor guys face just got redder and redder as we got onto the aircraft and sat next to each other, which presumably wasn't on the itinerary either.

"No, no, do not sit like that, please, you can't talk to each other" he pleaded once again.

We just nodded wisely and carried on talking.

Feeling a tiny bit sorry for Billy the Kid, we then discussed a compromise with him akin to hard negotiations at the heart of the United Nations. The end result involved us not budging in the slightest and him giving in on every single point in our favour. An excellent compromise Ingrid and I both felt!

I then called the air stewardess over for some vodka to celebrate the conclusion of the Billy peace talks.

"No, no please don't drink, please don't drink" he pleaded/begged/demanded.

We just nodded wisely and carried on talking.

Ingrid downed the first vodka as if it was a bottle of Ribena. I was more refined in my 3 gulps before the glass was empty strategy and Billy the Kid just sat across the aisle with his head in his hands knowing his career was over before it had even begun. As we flew towards the Greek sunshine, Ingrid and I laughed and laughed so much so that by half way I had become the world's expert on her ex-husband. My mastermind subject used to be me and now it would forever be Mr Chris Tarrant.

Billy, now not just at the end of his career, but at the end of his life, tried one last time to make us follow the 'rules', though with the rather surprising decision to try the very same tactics that he had used 58 times in the previous 3 hours since he had met us.

"Please, please don't talk about anything to do with husbands" he pleaded/begged/demanded again, which as I was now the world's leading expert on Mr Chris Tarrant Esq. and had already started to write his biography, was, to state the bleeding obvious, miles too late honey.

We just nodded wisely and carried on talking.

Then we did something I would like to think was an act of kindness that will stay in Billy's mind forever as he looks around for that new job. We offered him a vodka. It was a gesture of solidarity to join our gang, which let's face it was the cool gang to be with on the plane. After 2 seconds he gave in and downed one. And another. By the time we landed he was absolutely bloody hammered.

"Look, don't worry Billy" I said as we got off the plane, "we won't grass you up." Ingrid agreed. He just nodded in a I'm going to be really sick in a minute nodding type of way.

We carried him to the car waiting for us at the airport and went to the hotel which had been arranged for us to stay in before we would meet the rest of the ladies the next day. When we got there we again carried him in, carried him to his room and then we carried on the same chatting and drinking routine which had served us well so far at the bar of the hotel.

And my God did Billy the Kid look bad the next day! But jokes to one side, actually he did a great job with us in an impossible situation and is a real credit to the production company.

They are lucky to have him.

We took the ferry over to the Greek island which would be our home for the next 4 weeks, and it's fair to say we were full of girly excitement. That was until I saw Nando. She could barely look at me, and in fairness that probably was just only a tad worse than the scornful looks she was giving everyone else.

I decided later that day that I would remain as dignified as I could with her, but that was tested immediately when I looked out of my balcony window and saw her talking to the production team by the beach on the very first night. She was gesturing back to the house in that dramatic Latina gesturing way, and it was a certainty she wasn't telling them how much she was looking forward to spending a whole long month with me. Well that or she was moaning that her personal hairdresser and stylist hadn't arrived yet.

Whilst I secretly hoped all this meant she would be walking out of the show, the next morning she was still there at breakfast. When I asked the production team later, they told me she has a problem with you which was brutal honesty but I knew what was happening at least. I told them that from my side I would try and rise above it but the tension just kept getting worse as each hour passed, and when I returned from a trip to the mountains some days later with my knees all cut and my nails chipped, it reached a peak (before the next peak) when her cutting observation, in front of the whole group, was:

"Your nails were like that on day one darling. They are simply pathetic."

Torn between punching her with my pathetically nailed fist or continuing to rise above it, I remained dignified and just told her that

180

I agreed with her. Which usually totally throws someone looking for a fight to be honest, but to her she just took that as total vindication about what she was saying and how she was saying it.

So, yet again the rallying call arrived.

"Come on Cunders you can get through this."

Everyone on the show had to do some sort of task and mine was to run a restaurant for a night. Which I had always fancied doing as various family members had been in that trade. I was really excited about it until, that is, I gave Nando the task of being in charge of booze for the simple reason, well, she liked booze.

But when she heard the news after her already late arrival that night, she proclaimed to her subjects (e.g. us) "I don't open bottles my daaaarlings and a lady does not pour a drink for anyone. Ever."

Which call me old-fashioned is going to be a slight issue when your job is, well, to open bottles daaaarling and pour drinks for everyone.

To reinforce her point, she then stormed off to God knows where, leaving me and especially the restaurant owner in a state of fury. The owner was in the background all the time as these were real customers of his we were serving, and his reputation was therefore on the line. Now faced with the realisation that this civil war could affect his future trade (as the Greeks like their drink) he went positively mental.

"Who are you to do this to me!" he screamed at Nando as she walked away into the distance, "who are you?!" which at that split second I did then think about getting the whole restaurant to sing the football chant 'who are ya, who are ya' in solidarity, but amongst the chaos that was looming large, that probably wouldn't have helped things.

What didn't help things at the same time were customers turning up who had booked a table for 2, but actually meant a table for 11, as they had brought along granny and aunties to see what all the TV fuss was about. Greek hospitality apparently would not allow you to say 'On ya bike sunshine' so instead tables had to be found for them which only compounded the problems, as we needed someone to then pour the drinks for them.

But amazingly, out of the Mediterranean mist, out of the fading sunlight as night-time started to rear its mysterious head, a vision appeared. A Nancy vision. For some reason she had decided to come back and not just that she proclaimed she would actually also knuckle down and help, which she did. I could have fainted with happiness as I just wanted that evening to work out and her returning simply galvanised all of us. We finally bonded there and then, she mucked in and to her credit, made a really good go of it. Even the owner shut up for a bit and to make the miracle complete, Ingrid for the first time in 10 days also actually shut up for a while.

The evening was a success, as indeed for me I guess the whole show was.

I had been lying about my real age since my early modelling days and I had carried it on year after year, especially as I approached the horrible age of 50. On the Shirley show on the very first night at the beach, I revealed my true age to the other 7 ladies.

"I've got something to tell you all, I'm fifty today. I want to be happy with the real age I am."

And I was instantly relieved. For so long I had used bus numbers as my age, I was 37 for about 3 years, and then 45 every year since I was 48. Eamonn Holmes recently gave me 7 presents and apologised for missing my 38, 39, 41, 42, 44, 48 and 49th birthday's.

The whole month long experience did change my life, or at least clarify what I was beginning to already know about myself before I went out to Greece. When I returned from the filming in June 2018, I cut back on pointless nights out, not work nights but the other ones and have been far more selective on who I class as my friends. In the past I tended to try and help people who probably didn't deserve my help. The show made me realise who is good for me in my life and who is not. It was great because I didn't have my phone, all I had were my thoughts.

The Shirley Valentine Summer pushed me out of my celebrity comfort zone and tested me. Tested every part of my soul, tested if I actually did still like myself. And I do. I needed that at the very time in my life, I had doubt everywhere. It refreshed me. The celebrity wheel isn't important, the family wheel is. I was so desperate to see Josh and James at the end, it just heightened my love for them and reminded me that in life you never ever get off that wheel for your children, and indeed you never should want to.

Since doing the show I've grown up. Again. It hasn't worried me so much in the last 6 months being on/off single, because I've realised even more the importance of the real friendships that you make and spending quality time with people you actually like, not the ones you know are fake.

And I know how fake the celebrity world can be. The pretend friends will tell you that you look great, but as you go to freshen up they will say behind your back "She's dressed like Britney on a budget" and when you hear about that and question it, they deny it even to your face. I know that falseness comes in all walks of life, but in the showbiz world it is often what actually underpins it. It can make you lose your faith in human nature.

If I find a man to spend the rest of my life with of course that would be wonderful, but I'd rather be on my own than with someone who

I don't want to be with. I think that living a lie like that in a fake life of pretend is more lonely than actually being lonely. As my boys get older, they are still my total priority and will be forever, but they are obviously not going to hang around so much with me in the future and they are clever enough to fend for themselves now anyway. So, yes, I would really love to get married again and why not? I think I deserve that. I hope I deserve that. I am one of life's great romantics.

I now understand what an incredible life I have had so far and for the next instalment of it, I can do anything I want to, and life is just too damn short to not at least try. Warhol talked about 5 minutes of fame for everyone. The problem is, once you have had those 5 minutes you want another 5, then an hour, then a whole lifetime. I like being a celebrity I'm not going to deny that, and I have been lucky in that respect to be able to earn a living from it by being an extrovert.

I have always been a bit daring, it wasn't as if I was a nun and then took my top off suddenly to get promotion for a client. I just extended what I knew would work and it did. And yet I do not sleep around, I do not chase men, but it would be the perception in most people's eyes that I do. I would have the same perception too if I were you. I hope now you have read this book though, that is no longer the case and you see that I am just a hard worker, simple as that. I work at being me because I am good at being me, and me is what paid for my kids to grow up properly.

I had such an unbelievable response from people after the Valentine show, messaging me on Twitter and Instagram saying things like, "*I just ended it with my boyfriend, came back, watched the show and you've made me think there is hope.*" I'm so honoured that people could think like that, think that I have inspired them in some way and I hope love comes to them all in their lives. But love with a partner is just one part of life's wheel and I am blessed to have many good things in all the other areas. You rarely get a complete wheel.

Life deals you some cards and you play them as they come. It is never a perfect hand, you can't push for the cards you want, you can't force destiny to arrive in the way you want it to, at the precise moment you want it to. You just have to believe the dreams you seek can eventually arrive into your life, and if you have a good soul then they will.

Love's dangerous arrow will come to me again, and I'm better prepared for it this time when it does.

But there is another love. No one can properly describe the feeling a mother has for their children. You cannot put into words what comes from your inner soul. That is what they mean to me, that is why I have been 'Lizzie Cundy' for 10 years. I would not change a thing in that regard because I didn't crumble when their father walked out, and I got us through that period. It was down to me alone to do that and I did.

I am 50. I have my dignity, my wonderful experiences, my stories, my true friends and most of all I have Josh and James, who I have protected and cared for every single minute since they were born.

They are my life.

They are my love.

Bless you all for reading about the adventures I have been through. That, my darlings, for good or for bad, is the journey so far, and at the end of it I am no longer confused about who I want to be.

Miller or Cundy???? The debate has been settled in my mind.

Thank you and goodnight.

Lizzie has left the building.

Epilogue

"Lizzie took me to the X Factor final recently, last minute as usual, she had missed my birthday. It was so special hanging out with Simon Cowell, Robbie Williams and all the other stars backstage with her.

She is just one of Simon Cowell's gang! So connected in that world but trusted as part of the inner circle. I'm unbelievably proud of her for getting there.

The most special time for me on events like that is always afterwards when she drives me to the train station for my journey home. (Yes, celebrity Lizzie will drive her mates to the station). We finally get 10 minutes alone together. She moves from celebrity Lizzie, to just Lizzie Cundy Miller. It's simply the most precious time for me because it's when I get to see her true self.

I don't care about the celebrity world she is in, although it does have its perks with fabulous birthday treats, as above. I just care about her, as all her real friends, Josh and James do.

I admire her, respect her and love her."

Susie Homes (see The Romeo of Richmond chapter)

MASTERMIND

aka The Liz Quiz, aka are you a Cundy Junkie, aka fancy having a Cunty Punty?

So, by now you either know Lizzie quite well and it would be nice to know a bit more about her, or you don't care if you know her well or not, reading this book just passed the time by the pool or you didn't get to this page anyway, in which case you are probably one of Jason Cundy's friends!

But to end this book, a bit of juvenile distraction for you. A quiz. Come on run with it, it's fun. It could be worse, it could be a Lizzie dot-to-dot or a Lizzie spot the difference.

There are 35 questions below, you have to decide which one would Lizzie pick. It's one or the other, which would be her favourite?

The answers are on the last page. Now don't cheat, you know you are better than that.

For the record her sons Josh and James scored 28 and 25 respectively, Showbiz Simon 25 and Anthea Turner 23.

If you score 35

The police are on their way as you are frankly weird.

If you score 15 to 34

Not bad, but you should probably leave the house more and stop reading The Guardian.

If you score 6-15

Ok, you have only skim-read the book, but don't worry it is unlikely you will have to list this poor score in your CV for a job application like you do a degree, A levels etc.

If you score less than 5

You didn't get past the pictures section in this book, did you?

Choose one or the other:

THE ROLLING STONES or **THE BEATLES**
DURAN DURAN or **WHAM**
FAWLTY TOWERS or **ONLY FOOLS AND HORSES**
COFFEE or **TEA**
RUGBY or **FOOTBALL**
WINTER or **SUMMER**
RED WINE or **WHITE WINE**
CHICKEN or **BEEF**
CINEMA or **THEATRE**
STAR WARS or **LORD OF THE RINGS**
SHORT SKIRT or **TROUSER SUIT**
SEX or **LOVE**
CHRISTMAS DAY or **CHRISTMAS EVE**
BANANARAMA or **SPICE GIRLS**
SATURDAY NIGHT FEVER or **GREASE**
RED or **PINK**
PUB or **RESTAURANT**
YELLOW or **GREEN**
SALT or **PEPPER**
TOAST or **CEREAL**
ORANGE JUICE or **APPLE JUICE**
MEN IN JEANS or **MEN IN SUITS**
AUGUST or **DECEMBER**
STRICTLY or **I'M A CELEBRITY**
PINK or **PURPLE**
BEECH or **POOL**
DISCO or **PUNK**
TOMORROW or **TODAY**
CUDDLES or **SEX**
ELVIS or **SINATRA**
VEGAS or **NEW YORK**
BLACK or **RED**
3 or **7**
A BOOK or **A FILM**
8AM or **8PM**

What did Lizzie choose?

THE ROLLING STONES or <u>THE BEATLES</u>
DURAN DURAN or <u>WHAM</u>
<u>FAWLTY TOWERS</u> or ONLY FOOLS AND HORSES
COFFEE or <u>TEA</u>
RUGBY or <u>FOOTBALL</u>
WINTER or <u>SUMMER</u>
RED WINE or <u>WHITE WINE</u>
<u>CHICKEN</u> or BEEF
CINEMA or <u>THEATRE</u>
<u>STAR WARS</u> or LORD OF THE RINGS
SHORT SKIRT or <u>TROUSER SUIT</u>
SEX or <u>LOVE</u>
<u>CHRISTMAS DAY</u> or CHRISTMAS EVE
<u>BANANARAMA</u> or SPICE GIRLS
SATURDAY NIGHT FEVER or <u>GREASE</u>
<u>RED</u> or PINK
PUB or <u>RESTAURANT</u>
<u>YELLOW</u> or GREEN
SALT or <u>PEPPER</u>
TOAST or <u>CEREAL</u>
ORANGE JUICE or <u>APPLE JUICE</u>
MEN IN JEANS or <u>MEN IN SUITS</u>
<u>AUGUST</u> or DECEMBER
<u>STRICTLY</u> or I'M A CELEBRITY
<u>PINK</u> or PURPLE
<u>BEECH</u> or POOL
<u>DISCO</u> or PUNK
<u>TOMORROW</u> or TODAY
CUDDLES or <u>SEX</u>
<u>ELVIS</u> or SINATRA
<u>VEGAS</u> or NEW YORK
<u>BLACK</u> or RED
3 or <u>7</u>
A BOOK or <u>A FILM</u>
8AM or <u>8PM</u>

Photo credits:

Front cover
John Phillips / Stringer by Getty Images

Picture section 1
Page 17: Alan Strutt

Picture section 3
Page 20 (bottom): Mark Moody

For the first time in book publishing history, you can watch
the making of this book as Lizzie and Richard were filmed
at various stages during the writing process. None of the footage
was staged, it is raw film of their meetings as they craft the words
that finally end up in the book you have just read.

It's a fascinating 30 minute journey with laughter, emotion and
sometimes huge tension as they debate what should or should not
appear. This is groundbreaking voyeurism at its very best.

Just visit **www.talesfromtheredcarpet.com** and with two clicks
and £3.50* you can view the full documentary.

*A large glass of wine to drink whilst watching the film is optional and unfortunately
not included in the price. It is, however, recommended.*